# Leading
## THROUGH
# Change

SHEPHERDING THE
TOWN AND COUNTRY
CHURCH IN A NEW ERA

BARNEY WELLS | MARTIN GIESE | RON KLASSEN

ChurchSmart
RESOURCES

St. Charles, IL 60174
1-800-253-4276

Published by ChurchSmart Resources

We are an evangelical Christian publisher committed to producing excellent products at affordable prices to help church leaders accomplish effective ministry in the areas of church planting, church growth, church renewal and leadership development.

For a free catalog of our resources call 1-800-253-4276.

Cover design by: Julie Becker
Manuscript edited by: Stuart Hoffman

ISBN#: 1-889638-53-6

# Leading
# *THROUGH*
# Change

BARNEY WELLS | MARTIN GIESE | RON KLASSEN

# Dedications

To our wives and families, whose devotion to us and our town
and country ministries has remained unchanged through the years

and to

Jim Mason, who has been a mentor to the three of us
and exemplary in his unwavering lifelong commitment to
nurturing town and country churches.

# Acknowledgements

We would like to express our appreciation to the following:

Jim Mason, Don Green, and Ron Denlinger, who selflessly took time
to read our manuscript and provide invaluable feedback.

Dan Claussen, who gave us an entrée to our publisher.

Our respective ministries, which graciously
granted us time to work on the book.

Dave Wetzler and others at ChurchSmart, who provided their expertise
and encouragement, and who view publishing as a ministry.

Countless town and country pastors whom we have met through
the years who have inspired us, served as examples,
and processed our material with us.

# Contents

# Foreword

**THIS BOOK IS ABOUT CHANGE** in town and country churches. In today's society change is a given. Change will happen. Change is happening at an increasingly rapid pace, even in places where the prevailing notion is that "nothing new ever happens here." Change is.

Much change needs to be initiated in town and country churches today. Many town and country churches lack effective leaders. Many are not reaching unbelievers. Many show signs of stagnation and decline. Many have unkempt, outdated facilities reflecting sagging morale and an outdated ministry. In other words, many churches need to change.

Compounding the issue is that many pastors enter their communities trained to preach and offer pastoral care, but soon discover they need additional skills that will enable them to infuse new focus, vision, and motivation into their church. On the other end of the spectrum but equally challenging, some pastors enter their communities with considerable preparation for leading change, but soon find themselves in a heap of trouble because their preparation was not tailored for the town and country context.

This book, however, is not just about initiating change in the town and country church. Rural areas are experiencing changes that we are not seeking, and we are left with no choice but to respond to them. Change is. This book is about leading *through* change, whether it be proactive or reactive.

You might be facing issues such as these:

- Our community is changing but our church is not.
- Our church's worship style hasn't changed in recent memory.
- Because our church has not been keeping up with the times, we are not reaching young people.
- Our church is declining; we need to do something to turn it around.
- Newcomers to our church are bringing ideas that meet resistance and even create conflict.

- When I was called to serve this church as pastor, they asked me to bring change. Now they seem to oppose the very change they wanted.

- Our church building is run-down, unappealing, and almost impossible to work with. It sends the message that we are old, tired, and worn.

\* \* \* \* \* \* \* \* \* \*

Why this book when there are already many good books on change? Because we believe there are many change factors that are unique to town and country contexts:

- Change is unique in town and country contexts because it is happening in places where historically there has been little change.
- Change is unique in town and country contexts because of the complex web of relationships in each community. Should change lead to conflict, that conflict will affect not only my relationships in the church but also threaten the well-being of my bowling team, the extra help my daughter's teacher is giving her in school, and the hand my neighbor is quick to give me during harvest season—all because these folks are on the other side of the change. Many will conclude that maintaining good relationships is more important than change.
- Change is uniquely challenging in the town and country church because of the long-term shame that might come if it doesn't work. In a small town, this failure may cause me to be labeled for life. Because of this, I might wonder if the change is worth the risk to my reputation.
- Change is uniquely challenging because town and country churches, which are typically small, operate on low margins with little or no surplus to risk. If a church of 500 loses 5 people because they don't like a change, it's no big deal. But in a church of 50, a loss of 5 people is a big deal.
- Change is uniquely challenging in town and country churches because newcomers, often the pushers for change, may be looked upon with suspicion and even considered to be threats. One reason for this is that town and country people, at least until recently, have tended to be far less transient than city people. This

means they have a lot more invested in the church than their sub-urban counterpart. What right does a newcomer, who has almost nothing invested in the church, have to suggest change?

- Change may be more challenging in town and country areas because of the relative isolation from many goods, services, and opportunities. In an atmosphere with fewer options people are less accustomed to change.
- Change in town and country areas occurs at a slower pace than other contexts. Leading change requires more patience, more time.
- Change is elusive for many town and country pastors because their "job descriptions" are so sweeping that any desire to be a change agent is held prisoner by the urgent.
- Some changes coming to town and country contexts are not hap-pening in other places, such as the emergence of the new rural poor and the arrival of suburban transplants.
- Finally, some changes recommended in other books are not appropriate for town and country contexts. For instance, encour-aging formation of small groups may be desirable in city contexts. Yet, in a context of social intimacy where there is no place to hide, we might want to be cautious about implementing a small group format that strongly encourages transparency and vulnerability.

\* \* \* \* \* \* \* \* \* \*

What will happen to your church if you implement the suggestions in this book? Numerical growth could be an outcome, but that should not be your primary goal. In fact, some places are so isolated that there is limited potential for growth. While growth may be a by-product of change, it should not be the most important motive for change. The primary goals for change should be effectiveness and fruitfulness. This is our passion. Too many town and country churches have not seen significant positive changes happen in recent years. We should be alarmed by this. Eternal destinies are at stake. Personal growth and vitality are at stake. Church vitality is at stake, as is the community's. Should change not be happen-ing in your church, there may be no other church in the community to pick up the slack.

We have written this book for the hundreds of thousands of people who have been called to lead town and country churches through what we believe is the most challenging, exciting, demanding, and potentially productive era in history. We have written to equip and encourage, to inform and inspire. And yes, to prompt leaders and churches toward change.

## section one

# Town and Country Megatrends

**THIS FIRST SECTION DISCUSSES** significant changes in town and country areas. The trends we outline here are "mega" in town and country communities—massive changes that would lead most anyone who is familiar with them to conclude: "This is not your father's small town!"

Our primary goal in this section is to describe what we believe are noteworthy changes that have direct bearing upon town and country churches. Our purpose here is not primarily to suggest how to initiate or respond to change. Although this section does contain some practical suggestions, we're saving most of the "how-tos" for Section Two.

**CHAPTER ONE**

# Change Is

**BOB SWENSON HAS LIVED IN MILLERSVILLE** and been a part of Fox Creek Church all of his life. His parents and grandparents are buried in the local cemetery. Things in his town and church have been pretty much the same through all the years. There has been little change.

The first sign that change was in the wind came at a church business meeting. Bob had been the treasurer for as long as almost anyone could remember. His financial report was always something like this: "We've taken in about $2,150. We spent $1,940, maybe $1,950. All the bills are paid, and we've got a little to tide us over." For years this kind of reporting suited everyone just fine.

Then Jeremy Morrison raised his hand at a meeting. Jeremy had moved to Millersville about a year earlier to fill the business manager position at the recently built snowmobile manufacturing plant on the edge of town. He asked, "Would it be possible to have a written, itemized report?"

Bob was more than a little perturbed by the question. He felt that Jeremy didn't trust him. But after the meeting a friend reassured him. "Jeremy didn't mean anything by that suggestion. That's just his business background coming through. I tell you what, my wife works in an office where she produces financial reports. If you give her the church checkbook before the next business meeting, she can write up a report for you." Bob reluctantly agreed. Maybe a written report wouldn't be such a bad idea, he thought.

About a year later someone else suggested, "Maybe we need more than one person to count the church offerings."

That sealed it for Bob. He was devastated to discover that some-one—in fact, a brother in Christ—didn't trust him. Why, he would have starved before he took even a penny of the Lord's money! Bob resigned. He still comes to church, and still sits in his usual place, but he's just not the same.

This is just one example of change coming to town and country churches. And, as Bob's experience illustrates, many changes come hard. It could be that some in the church are reluctant to quit using the organ, and not so much because they think it's the only appropriate instru-ment for the worship services but because it was given in memory of a respected parishioner. It could be that some are reluctant to change the Sunday morning service format, not because they personally are unwilling to see change but because they fear how some will respond. Yet they feel tension, knowing that if the church doesn't change its worship services a number of folks are threatening to pull out and start a new church. It could be that some are hesitant to change the Sunday service's starting time, even though that time was established decades ago to accommodate dairy farmers, and the last dairy in the community sold out 20 years ago. It could be that some are resistant to replacing worn, hard pews with com-fortable and practical chairs.

This is a sampling of changes that have created challenges in town and country churches in recent years. It also hints at some of the reasons why many changes happen. All the changes mentioned above were prob-ably motivated by one or more of the following factors.

## Dissatisfaction

Are you driving a car that you bought used? Many reading this prob-ably are. How were you able to find a perfectly functional used car to buy? Why don't people who buy new cars drive them until they are ready for the junk heap? Dissatisfaction.

Dissatisfaction is the unfavorable comparison of the current situation with an alternative one. Automobile manufacturers spend millions of dol-lars every year to create it. You may be quite pleased with your current car and have no thought of needing a new one, until you see a television com-mercial. Suddenly the admirable and dependable qualities of your current vehicle begin to dim in your thinking, and the features of the new car seem increasingly more desirable. You have become dissatisfied.

Dissatisfaction happens in the town or country church when a new-comer decides that the children's program in his former church is better.

It comes when the recent MBA graduate returns to his roots and lets it be known that the church's financial record keeping isn't being done according to widely accepted business practices. It comes because town and country residents are not nearly as provincial as they once were, and in their travels they encounter churches with different worship formats. It comes when a church member moves to a suburb and reports back how pleased she is that her new church has a gym. Dissatisfaction-motivated change starts when someone is able to envision a more desirable alternative.

Often pastors and leaders can use dissatisfaction for good. Other times it can be used unwisely. Sure enough, change happens—the pastor's address changes! Sometimes members leave. Change has its hazards. Hopefully this book will help you avoid a few of them.

### Discomfort

Let's do a little experiment. Put a clock in front of you and sit perfectly motionless. When you can't sit still any longer because your nose itches or your muscles feel cramped, go ahead and move. Look at the clock. How long were you motionless? If you are like most, you did well to last two minutes. Sitting motionless for very long produces discomfort, and when the level of discomfort becomes intolerable, change occurs.

Discomfort is what makes people willing to quit a job they dislike and take a lesser-paying job in a small town. Discomfort is what prompts people to decide to get out of the city, away from freeways that are more like parking lots, away from all the hassles that go with being surrounded by throngs of people, though they have no idea what country living is like. Discomfort leads a church to build or start a second service when its sanctuary becomes crowded. Discomfort is the primary motivator behind doing something about 100-year-old, rickety, back-breaking pews, even though there's a lot of history associated with those pews. Discomfort spurs the church to add new bathrooms just off the foyer upstairs, realizing that George is having trouble navigating the stairs to the basement and will have to quit coming if something isn't done soon.

Discomfort too has its perils. Change driven by discomfort may be a leap into the unknown, with the assumption—sometimes mistaken—that anything has to be better than what is. For example, more than one church has rushed into changing its constitution or bylaws, and found the resulting governance structure even worse than the one it replaced. Discomfort may also motivate pastors to resign and leave a frustrating situation on the assumption that any other church will be an improvement over their present one.

### Coercion

Coercion is the use of physical, economic, political, or religious power to force an undesired change. When you are in a hurry but you slow down to the speed limit because you see your county sheriff parked on the side of the road, you are experiencing coercion by political (and economic!) power.

Coercion happens in the town and country church when a member threatens to withhold support, knowing that his contributions comprise 25 percent of the total church budget. It happens when a faction threatens to leave if they do not get their way—the faction knowing that the already small church will do almost anything to avoid losing a third of its membership. Coercion even occurs in the form of physical power in some colorful and heartfelt church discussions. Coercion is usually not an appropriate means of producing change in the church. An exception would be situations of church discipline where it is biblically mandated.

### Displacement    Air force moves

A tornado whipped across the prairie and flattened the building of the church Ron pastored in Corn, Oklahoma. In a matter of seconds, the church was displaced.

Displacement happens when something uninvited forces change. When a new interstate highway splits a family farm. When a military base closes near a small town. When a downtown hotel closes because the federal government decided to move the main highway to the edge of town. When a farmer is forced to sell out because wheat prices remain too low. When loved ones are lost through death. Displacement seldom produces desired change. Unlike coercion, which is intentional and may be resisted, displacement is irresistible. Once displacement occurs, change inevitably follows.

The town or country church that experiences displacement *will* change. It has no choice. We know of a century-old country church building that was struck by lightning and burned to the ground. Lightning forced the church into a building program, though some didn't want change because of emotional ties to the old building. (See the epilogue for this unusual story.) When the small church's main leader dies suddenly, major disruption occurs while the church struggles to fill the void. If a major employer in the area shuts down, the economy will be affected and church attendance will decrease as residents are forced to move away to find work. These displacement outcomes are not intended and are seldom welcomed. (Well, okay, a few were happy when that old church sanctuary was struck by lightning!) Displacement is a strong motivator of change.

## Leading Through Change

We share these four motivators to show that many changes that occur in town and country churches are not caused by deliberate planning. These changes come not because church leaders *make* them happen. Rather, they come in much more spontaneous, unplanned, even haphazard fashion, usually caused by at least one of the four factors mentioned above and often by a combination of two or more.

While later in this book we want to talk about *making* change happen, we want to first address changes that *are* happening in many town and country settings. You're not making these changes happen. You don't necessarily want them to happen. But they are happening, and you can't do anything to stop them. Such is the nature of much change. In fact, in our new millennium we are in the midst of countless changes, more than this world has ever seen. In today's society change is a given. Change will happen. Change is.

In order to lead the town and country church through change, we must first understand the forces that cause change and what kinds of change they are causing. We must understand that, while there are changes that are initiated by leaders, many forces behind change are unintended and even unwanted. If we are going to be good shepherds of the flock the Lord has entrusted to us, we must not only *lead* change, we must also lead *through* change. We must respond appropriately to the changes coming our way that are not of our making and out of our control. Leading *through* change is essential for the church to carry out its mission.

The next four chapters discuss four major changes that are happening that we need to lead *through*. Perhaps not all are happening in your community. If not, you have our permission to skip that chapter and go on to the next, though we're hoping that curiosity will get the best of you and you'll read it anyway. Plus, it is possible that a change is happening but it is so subtle or slow that you are not conscious of it.

We'll start by talking about newcomers who have moved into the area.

CHAPTER TWO

# Land of Opportunity

## *The change: Newcomers moving in*

**DAVE NELSON WAS TIGHT-LIPPED** when he stood and spoke at the congregational meeting at Oak Grove Church. He, his wife, and their two small children had moved into the community just a few months before and had recently joined the church. "I think we need to pave the parking lot," Dave said. "Last Sunday I was carrying my children into church in the rain, and the mud went over my shoes. Not only is a muddy parking lot an inconvenience, it also makes a poor first impression for visitors." Many heads were nodding as Dave spoke.

From the corner near the door, sitting in his regular spot, Ruddy Morris responded. "How can we even think about paving our parking lot when so many other needs are more important? Our church has gotten along just fine without a paved parking lot since its beginning more than 80 years ago. Instead of being concerned about our own shoes, we should be discussing how we might give more money to others."

Ruddy sat down and reflected on his growing frustration. Discussions like this were becoming more frequent. And, they were clearly being initiated by the newcomers. First it had been a family or two. He had been excited to see some new blood in the church. But then a few more families had moved into the area and started attending. They were buying up perfectly good farmland and building expensive houses. *Where in the world do they get all that money?* Ruddy wondered. *Things are clearly getting out of hand. Before long these newcomers will outnumber us old-timers and we'll be paving the parking lot instead of giving money to people who are starving in Africa.*

## Enter: Newcomers

Many living in rural communities today didn't grow up there. Newcomers are rapidly moving in. Numerous town and country areas are growing at a pace that exceeds many suburbs. This has turned rural areas into a Land of Opportunity. This opportunity extends to the church. For many years a disproportionately large number of missionaries have been sent out by rural churches. Now the mission field is coming to them!

Why so many newcomers? There are many reasons. Some are moving to the country because of a host of alluring movies and books depicting idealized rural settings: breath-taking scenery, a "Norman Rockwellesque" kind of atmosphere, a preconceived image of "wholesome country living." Some are seeking a lower cost of living. Some are in computer-related occupations that, because of technological advances in recent years, allow them to live anywhere in the world they desire—quite a contrast to years gone by when people had to move to the cities where the jobs were. Others are looking for a peaceful setting in which to retire. Yet others are following the job trail of new industries that are springing up in the country: tourism, light manufacturing, landfills, prisons, and others. There is much diversity today in rural communities, so much so that "rural" can no longer be equated with "farming."

Communities that cater to the expectations of outsiders or that are well located are more likely to grow:

- Communities that offer extras, such as recreational opportunities (parks, golf courses, hiking, pools, scenic surroundings, etc.).
- Communities with schools that have good reputations.
- Communities with easy access to larger population centers, thereby attracting the commuters and those who want to live in the country but still be within close reach of all the amenities of the city.
- Communities that are focusing on economic development, offering small business employment opportunities and attracting the chain stores that tend to be the first to show up in small towns (e.g., Subways, Caseys convenience stores, Dollar General Stores).

Some of the newcomers are urbanites fleeing the city, getting away from the hectic pace of urban living with its traffic jams, air pollution, and high crime rates. Some are from a different economic class, either richer or poorer (chapter four further discusses these newcomers). Some are from a different ethnic group. Newcomers of all stripes are finding their way to town and country areas.

Whoever the newcomers, they are different from the traditional rural residents. Their arrival changes things. They may be welcome to some, but not to others. Their ways may or may not be accepted. For many, their arrival is viewed as a mixed blessing. Long-time residents realize that newcomers offer hope for the future. They know their community has been suffering decline for many years and will eventually die unless outsiders move in. But they wish these outsiders were more like them. Not being like them often leads to conflict, such as depicted in the story that opened this chapter.

Church leaders in smaller communities might do well to look through their local phone book and analyze who is in their community. In larger communities you might get this information from a variety of other sources (we talk more about this in chapter six). It is quite possible that newcomers may have snuck into the community unnoticed! Have these newcomers made their way into the church? If not, why not? Very possibly the answer can be summed up in two words: cultural collision.

## Cultural Collision

Newcomers to town and country areas are a culturally mixed bag. They are culturally diverse. They are culturally conflicted, not only in relation to the traditional rural residents but also within themselves.

Many newcomers want rural folksiness but also desire professionalism. They like spontaneity but look for organization. They like the relaxed nature of town and country people but seek perfectionism. They are drawn to the quaintness of the past but want certain things to be up-to-date. They are conflicted within themselves.

The newcomers' arrival also causes considerable conflict with others, particularly the long-term residents. These conflicts stem from a different way of thinking, a different cultural orientation, even a different vocabulary. This is humorously illustrated by the following conversation between Cowboy Joe and his friends who are reflecting on his first visit to a big-city church and trying to adjust to the new lingo.

"When I got there, they had me park my old truck in the corral," Joe began.

"You mean the parking lot," interrupted Charlie, a more city-wise fellow.

"Then I walked up the trail to the door," Joe continued.

"The sidewalk to the door," Charlie corrected him.

"Inside the door I was met by this dude," Joe went on.

"That would be the usher," Charlie explained.

"Well, the usher led me down the chute," Joe said.

"You mean the aisle," Charlie said.

"Then he led me to a stall and told me to sit there," Joe continued.

"Pew," Charlie responded.

"Yeah," recalled Joe, "that's what that pretty lady said when I sat down beside her."

*different perspectives*

Long-term residents and newcomers have different perspectives! They are on different wavelengths. It can be hard for them to understand each other. Lack of understanding often leads to conflict.

Because of the likelihood of misunderstanding and conflict between newcomers and long-term residents, the remainder of this chapter presents possible differences between what we are going to call the agrarian and cosmopolitan cultures. We've chosen the word *Agrarian* to describe those who have always lived in the country. *Cosmopolitan* refers to the collection of newcomers that are moving into rural areas from a variety of walks of life.

Just understanding some of the differences between agrarians and cosmopolitans should provide considerable help. We'll also insert some suggestions that may aid you as a leader in helping these people to peacefully coexist and even grow to appreciate and value each other.[1]

| Category | Agrarians | Cosmopolitans |
|----------|-----------|---------------|
| Success | Survival | Advancement |

Because of ongoing economic hardship and other crises regularly encountered by agrarians—such as fluctuating markets (sometimes drastically so), bad weather, cattle diseases, and crop failures—they may define success as "making it another year." Many of their friends have not

---

[1] The authors would like to acknowledge the contribution of Dr. Gary Goreham of the Department of Sociology/Anthropology at North Dakota State University in the early development of our thinking concerning Agrarian and Cosmopolitan Contrasts, and the impact of these contrasts in the arena of change.

made it, which makes their survival an achievement. But for many cosmopolitans, surviving is not good enough. Success to them is when this year's sales exceed the last. Taking this perspective into the church, they often see success in terms of measurable progress such as increased attendance and giving, and the addition of programs.

A newcomer pastor who is not from an agrarian background may struggle with a "survival is success" mentality, in part because church growth books place his "plateaued" church in an unfavorable category.[2] If the church does not respond to his ideas for progress, he may take this as personal rejection; however, the real problem is probably different cultural orientations.

Pastors or leaders who find themselves in a survival-is-success congregation need to first affirm survival. To say, "All we are doing is surviving," is to not understand the agrarian culture that views survival as the pinnacle of a pyramid, in contrast to cosmopolitans who view it as the foundation of a pyramid upon which are built more ambitious goals. Instead of minimizing survival, leaders should applaud it: "Praise God, we've survived!" Then they can further say, "God must still have a purpose for us. Let's move forward!" And then they can nudge the church toward measurable areas of progress.

If the pace of progress in the town and country church seems too slow, pastors and church members might consider taking loops of ministry that extend beyond the local context: Go on a mission trip. Work with a parachurch ministry. Write a book. Help plant a church in a neighboring town. Many rural Christians have ministries that extend beyond their local church. This not only helps relieve their frustration of being in a static church, but also means they can come back to the church and share what God has done through them, which may encourage others in the congregation to move out of their survival mode.

---

[2] In recent years church growth writers have often quoted the statistic that more than 80 percent of churches in America are plateaued or in decline, the implication being that these churches are not healthy. The statistic cited does not take into account that thousands upon thousands of churches are located in town and country communities with declining populations, where corresponding statistical decline is virtually inevitable in the church. Such a generalization, made without considering this demographic phenomenon, has unnecessarily added to the discouragement that many are facing in town and country churches today.

| Category | Agrarians | Cosmopolitans |
|----------|-----------|---------------|
| Size | Small is beautiful | Big is better |

Small is attractive to most agrarians. Large might be threatening. One reason they are likely to fight school consolidation is because they do not believe bigger is better. They may have similar mixed feelings about growth in their church. Many cosmopolitans, on the other hand, see a direct correlation between a church's size and its vitality. Just as bigger stores offer more choices, so do bigger schools and churches. Thus bigger is better and growth is important. This is an example, by the way, of how newcomers to rural communities are conflicted within themselves. They move to a smaller place because small is attractive to them; however once there, they want things to be bigger!

Church leaders need to make sure their theology is right. God does not view small as inferior and neither should we (e.g., Deuteronomy 7:7-8, Zechariah 4:10a). Leaders need to make sure they do not speak condescendingly when using the word "small." A smaller youth group is not, of necessity, inferior. In fact, there are certain dynamics that can only take place in a smaller group setting. Fewer worshipers does not, of necessity, mean inferior worship. Some of the most meaningful worship happens in intimate contexts. Might the fact that small has its advantages be why many large churches work hard at finding ways to be small? Is it a coincidence that the small-group movement has coincided with the megachurch movement?

Because cosmopolitans have chosen to move to rural turf, perhaps they need to be gently reminded from time to time that a major reason they moved out of the city is because they thought small is better. And, perhaps church leaders' greater focus should be on church health rather than numerical growth. Hopefully the growth will come, as it often does, even in sparsely populated areas.

| Category | Agrarians | Cosmopolitans |
|----------|-----------|---------------|
| Community | Independent | Interdependent |

Agrarians and cosmopolitans often differ in their approach to community. Historically, agrarians are independent, likely due to their isolation. Today they continue to be protective of that independence.

Cosmopolitans, by contrast, tend to be more interdependent. They are more accustomed to working together to achieve strategic goals.

For agrarians, interdependence and cooperative effort are concessions they make only for survival. When an essential task is too big or complex to accomplish independently, they will form a temporary alliance to see it done. In the past, barn raisings and threshing bees reflected this: "If you help me build my barn, I'll help you build your barn and we will both survive."

Today, agrarians are still very willing to be "neighborly" in times of crisis or need, but may have difficulty cooperating when the crisis or need has passed. Within their local church, agrarians may help one another when calamity strikes but may not be so cooperative when serving on a standing committee.

Cosmopolitans, while perhaps not as neighborly as their agrarian counterparts, are more accustomed to working interdependently to achieve strategic goals. In a complex urban environment, this is essential for achievement. Within a local church, cosmopolitans are apt to be more comfortable with group process.

Many agrarians view working with others as a last resort. Cosmopolitans, on the other hand, view interdependence as a first resort in a strategic plan to accomplish a mutually beneficial goal. Agrarians cooperate to survive; cosmopolitans cooperate to achieve.

| Category | Agrarians | Cosmopolitans |
|----------|-----------|---------------|
| Planning | Presumptuous | Essential |

On the farm there are constant reminders of limitations and inability to control surroundings, because of unpredictability due to factors beyond one's control. We already listed some of these factors under "Success" above—like the unpredictable behavior of animals, crop failures, bad weather, and fluctuating markets. In contrast, cosmopolitans live and work in controlled environments, for example: precision manufacturing, technology that operates like clockwork, room temperatures set by thermostats, regular paychecks. Consequently they live with the assumption (agrarians would say "illusion") that they are in control of life.

These two vastly different environments may spawn key differences between how agrarians and cosmopolitans think. For instance, with so many uncertainties, establishing vision and setting goals—the subject of numerous books and seminars in recent years—may be regarded by agrarians as presumptuous, foolish, and perhaps even sinful. How can we make plans when, as stated in James 4:13-16, we don't know what tomorrow will bring? What if the wheat harvest is a total loss? But cosmopolitans also have verses, such as 1 Corinthians 9:24-27, to back up their conviction that planning, vision, and goal setting are essential for a sense of direction and purpose, and for progress and success.

These differing perspectives can be balanced by realizing that agrarians do set goals. They have things in mind to do for the day, as well as an idea of how much land they would like to eventually farm and how big they would like their cattle herd to become. But they tend to hold these goals loosely and somewhat privately.

Church leaders in this kind of context can find ways to satisfy both the agrarian and cosmopolitan perspectives. Leaders can set private goals for themselves. They can work with the congregation to establish flexible goals that can easily be adjusted or postponed should something like a crop failure happen. These goals might best be kept informal, rather than carefully scripted. And the whole concept of vision should probably remain more subtle and low-key.

| Category | Agrarians | Cosmopolitans |
|---|---|---|
| Perfectionism | Jacks-of-all-trades | Specialists |

Agrarians tend to be jacks-of-all-trades but masters-of-none. Their work requires that they be a welder, carpenter, plumber, mechanic, electrician, farmer, trucker, livestock handler, commodities trader, accountant—the list goes on and on. This means they cannot possibly be proficient in all things. And so, rather than ask, "Can I do the job well?" agrarians ask, "Can I do the job well enough?" This doesn't mean one cannot find perfectionists among agrarians; it just means that one cannot possibly fill all of these roles as adeptly as a specialist who fills only one of the roles.

Cosmopolitans are generally more accustomed to specialization. They tend to do fewer things, which often means they do those fewer things well. Then they hire experts to do what they cannot do, and these people, being specialists, also do a quality job. Cosmopolitans resonate with the Wizard of Id cartoon that in one frame shows a sign that reads "Podiatrist" and in the next frame "Right foot only."

This contrast could create friction. Agrarians' approach to ministry might be, "We'll do the best we can." They will likely be satisfied with an adequate keyboard player, whereas a cosmopolitan may be satisfied with nothing less than a high level of ability. Agrarians will likely be satisfied with financial record keeping that was done as well as the church treasurer knew how, whereas cosmopolitans will likely be looking for computer-generated reports and bar graphs. Agrarians may not complete church maintenance projects quite as proficiently as a specialist would, but they are thinking, "At least we didn't have to hire it done." Cosmopolitans, meanwhile, continually find their eyes drifting toward the mitered pieces of wood trim that don't quite fit together like they should.

Wise pastors and church leaders will realize that the agrarian perspective has more to applaud than condemn. A willingness to serve is better than a "Let's hire it done" mentality. Participation is usually a higher virtue than perfectionism. At the same time it is good for pastors and church leaders to, in a gentle and noncondescending manner, nudge their people in the direction of quality.

| Category | Agrarians | Cosmopolitans |
|----------|-----------|---------------|
| Finances | Uncertain income | Steady income |

Few things are more baffling to cosmopolitans than the agrarian's approach to finances. For one thing, an agrarian might think others are far better off financially than he, not because they make more money but because they have a regular paycheck.

Cosmopolitans don't understand the "poor-rich" farmer. That's because farmers' asset-to-income ratio is generally imbalanced. Though they have considerable assets, they may live at near-poverty level, often because their assets are nonliquid and nonmonetary (land, machinery, livestock). When there is a money crunch at church, the cosmopolitans might wonder why the agrarians don't sell a cow to help out. But agrarians are reluctant to do so because the cow is their source of income. On the other hand, agrarians may have a hard time understanding why cosmopolitans invest so much in their homes, not realizing their homes represent a primary part of their net worth.

Because life is unpredictable and income not guaranteed, agrarians tend to find ways to get by and save for a rainy day. They do not view excess funds as excess because sooner or later they will be needed. Agrarians tend to spend only what's absolutely needed. They are more likely to fix broken plumbing than spend money on paving the parking lot. *Budget* is a foreign term to some agrarians. How can income be budgeted when no one knows what the price of calves will be this fall? Budgeting may be viewed as presumptuous or an exercise in futility.

| Category | Agrarians | Cosmopolitans |
| --- | --- | --- |
| Outlook on life | Pessimistic | Optimistic |

Frequent disappointments can produce a pessimistic outlook. This is the agrarian's defense mechanism, a protection against dashed hopes. It works this way: If they expect the worst, then whatever happens isn't so bad. Say "Good morning!" to a farmer and the farmer might guardedly reply, "Oh, I don't know. It looks like rain." To which you might respond, "That'd be great for the crops." The farmer's response: "Might drown us out." A farmer seemingly never expects a profitable year. Yet, at the same time farmers are some of the most optimistic people around, as evidenced by the fact they keep putting a crop in the ground no matter how many times they've been hailed out or how low the price of wheat is.

Cosmopolitans might tire of the agrarians' negative outlook, tire of a "But what if?" mentality, tire of a hesitancy to take risks—even when times are good. They need to understand why agrarians tend to be more chronically pessimistic and not allow the agrarians' pessimism to become their pessimism. Church leaders also need to make sure the church is an oasis in the desert of discouragement. And, while sympathetic to the agrarians' outlook, they should not allow it to impede the progress of the church or put a damper on the church's optimism.

| Category | Agrarians | Cosmopolitans |
| --- | --- | --- |
| Time | Almanac | DayTimer® |

Even if by personality agrarians are time oriented, the nature of their work forces them to be task oriented: "First I'll do chores, then run to town for repairs, then fix the bailer, then go a few rounds in the field." This task orientation often is due to imprecise timing because of factors beyond their control. It is impossible, for instance, to anticipate the behavior of animals and schedule accordingly. Rounding up cattle may take an hour or half a day.

To strike up a conversation, someone asked an agrarian child: "How old are you?"

"Five."

"When do you turn six?"

"When my daddy plants corn again."

If the church needs a new roof, in response to the question of when, the agrarian will say, "After planting." When is that? Answer: "When it's done." This can be frustrating for cosmopolitans who carry a DayTimer® and plan their calendar many days ahead and in 15-minute increments. (We know one cosmopolitan pastor in an agrarian community who budgets eight minutes a day for unexpected phone calls!) An agrarian might show up late to a meeting saying, "I had one more round to go in the field." Church leaders would probably be wise to not make an issue of this task orientation. To some degree, timeliness is cultural. To many agrarians, 7:00 p.m. means "more or less around that time."

Many pastors plan their work by the clock. But agrarians are not likely to understand if they can't see the pastor because it's "the pastor's time to study." The farmer might live 40 miles away, and this is the time when he needs to come to town and while in town he needs to drop in and talk to his pastor.

| Category | Agrarians | Cosmopolitans |
|----------|-----------|---------------|
| Work | Manual | Mental |

A new pastor was assisting in a feed store, helping to fill sacks with corn. As he pulled his first bag off the scale and started to close it, the pastor noticed a look of concern on the face of the store owner. "When we tie sacks, we use a miller's knot," the owner said. "I don't suppose you can do that." He had forgotten that his pastor had farmed for 10 years. When he easily tied the knot the store owner was impressed. "You're the first preacher I ever saw," he told him, "who knew anything at all about working."

An agrarian is likely to define "real" work as manual labor. Desk work, or mental work, may not be viewed with the same respect. Cosmopolitans, on the other hand, might think Manual Labor is the President of Mexico! They can be real klutzes when it comes to doing physical work, either because they aren't accustomed to it or because they don't have the muscle or stamina for it.

Cosmopolitan pastors may not understand why they are accused by agrarians of not working hard. This can be a threat to their credibility. This difference in perspective can be eased if pastors get out of the study from time to time and do some manual labor. As they earn credibility, they can back off from physical labor and devote more time to pastoral ministry.

| Category | Agrarians | Cosmopolitans |
|----------|-----------|---------------|
| People | Relationships | Roles |

Agrarians tend to think in terms of how they relate to each other, as opposed to functions and titles. Cosmopolitans might say, "He chairs our church board. He is a senior partner in a law firm and also serves on the town council." But agrarians will probably think of people in terms of relationships: "This is Bob, Jim and Nadine's boy. He lives down at the old McPherson place."

A cosmopolitan pastor may think his people care about his degrees, theological expertise, and career experience, when in reality what they care most about is how he relates to them. He needs to, as quickly as possible, work himself into the web of relationships by doing things like attend ball games, go to parties and celebrations, invite people over, visit elderly shut-ins, go to cattle sales, join the volunteer fire department, and frequent the coffee shop. Having impact in a rural community doesn't just happen when the pastor fulfills his official duties; relational bonding is also necessary.

| Category | Agrarians | Cosmopolitans |
|----------|-----------|---------------|
| Decision making | Grassroots | Top-down |

Because they are more informal and less structured, agrarians tend to view committee and congregational meetings as opportunities for fellowship. Dialogue will drift from the business at hand. Ultimately decisions will likely be made informally. This may not settle well with cosmopolitans who believe meetings should have an established agenda, focused discussion, motions, and votes.

Agrarians are accustomed to being "CEOs" in their business. This means they are involved in every decision, great or small. But if this method of decision making is evident in the church, then cosmopolitans, who are accustomed to giving and following orders in the workplace, may react with frustration at the seemingly petty issues that are brought up in meetings.

Some agrarians are reluctant to talk in public meetings, perhaps because they don't want to risk conflict. After all, they have to live with each other the rest of the week! Thus it is likely that some decisions will be made apart from the meeting through an informal but carefully worked out way of exploring how everyone feels. Often these grassroots informal meetings convene in the church foyer, on the phone, in the cafe, or on the street. While agrarians may give assent to formal decision-making processes, they don't put a lot of stock in those processes. Any formal way of arriving at a decision can be rendered meaningless by informal discussions.

Cosmopolitans might get frustrated when their agrarian counterparts easily approve a decision at a meeting, only to later hear them complain about it, ignore it, or reverse it. Church leaders are wise to first talk about ideas and issues informally, letting people come to a consensus, then bring the issue to a meeting and a vote. Chapter eight addresses this further.

### General Solutions to Tensions

Leaders who find themselves in the midst of agrarian/cosmopolitan differences would do well to continually remind themselves and their congregation that neither way of thinking is necessarily wrong. Rather, each way of thinking is just different from the other. Each is a reflection of its culture. Leaders can go a long way in diffusing tensions simply by helping each culture understand the other and by helping each value the other's way of thinking.

Leaders may want to address these differences through informal discussions. Agrarians are more likely to accept newcomers and adapt to some of their ways if, in dialogue, they wrestle with questions like, "Why do you suppose newcomers who visit aren't staying in our church? How would God view the spiritual needs of these newcomers? What do you suppose He would want us to do to reach them? What will eventually happen to our church if we don't open our doors to newcomers?"

Similarly, a lot can be gained through informal discussions with cosmopolitans: "Try to put yourself in their shoes. How do you think long-term residents might feel about having newcomers moving in? What kind of attitude would the Bible encourage us to have toward the old-timers?

What are the characteristics that attracted you to this community?"

In more public contexts, as in Sunday school classes or from the pulpit, it would be good for leaders to help people in the church understand the demographic changes that are happening around them and help people see it is these changes that are exposing cultural differences. Use basic principles from Cultural Anthropology 101: "How do you suppose the [name a missionary family known in your church] had to adapt when they went to Africa? Now that the mission field is moving in here, what might God want us to do to reach these different people for Christ?" There are endless texts to share from God's Word that can help: texts that encourage us to submit to one another (Ephesians 5:21), to "become a Jew in order to win Jews" (1 Corinthians 9:20), to do all we can to live at peace with others (Romans 12:18), to have new and flexible wineskins to accommodate new wine (Matthew 9:17), to have the kinds of attitudes that enable us to live in unity with each other (Ephesians 4:2-3). These kinds of teaching will help people posture themselves differently. Many honestly don't realize they are wrestling with cultural differences; they think they are defending the faith or dealing with obstinate people.

In communities that are growing, the arrival of newcomers brings its set of challenges. The arrival of newcomers presents new opportunities for ministry. Leaders should be thankful for this new mission field and tackle the challenges with eagerness and wisdom.

But while some communities are growing, others are not. In fact, some are experiencing considerable decline. The next chapter addresses this equally challenging change.

CHAPTER THREE

# What's Up Down on the Farm?

## _The change: Depopulation_

**WHILE MANY TOWN AND COUNTRY AREAS** are brimming with growth and optimism, this scenario is not true everywhere. The change that is happening in many such communities is not growth but depopulation—particularly those that are heavily dependent on agriculture and those that are located a considerable distance from larger population centers.

The population in agricultural-dependent communities has declined almost everywhere in the United States and Canada. Whereas 80 to 100 years ago about one-third of the population were farmers, today this number has shrunk to a mere two percent. Farm equipment has gotten much bigger and considerably more high-tech through the years, resulting in drastically less manpower needed. At the same time, farm commodity prices have remained flat for decades, not even keeping up with inflation, forcing many farmers out of business and—due to lower profit margins—forcing other farmers to increase the size of their operations.

Twenty-four years ago when Barney arrived at his country church, only two in the congregation were not in farm-related jobs: a lawyer and Barney. Today less than 20 percent of the church is in an agricultural business. Each of the authors has grieved on many occasions with those who have lost their farms or related jobs. We're certain that many of you can identify with this situation.

What's true on the farm has also been true with other agrarian occupations. Many coal and iron mines have shut down across the country, due to such things as environmental concerns and foreign competition. Mines that remain open have far fewer laborers, due to better equipment replacing the need for manpower. Many foresting operations have met similar fates.

Remote towns are not receiving the influx of people that towns closer to cities are experiencing. Most of the folks who are moving to the country want to be within easy driving distance of a city. The exodus of agrarians in remote communities coupled with a lack of transplants from the cities to replace them is a recipe for decline.

Other small towns have declined due to a factory closing, or the interstate highway bypassing the town, or the railroad going elsewhere. There are many reasons why a considerable number of rural communities are experiencing decline. In many places, half the businesses on Main Street are boarded up. Buildings are run-down. The only traffic jams occur when two vehicles facing opposite directions are parked in the middle of the road with the drivers behind the wheels talking to each other.

Section Two will address ways you can lead through changes such as depopulation. But because of special circumstances that relate to decline, we want to provide some help and encouragement before going any further.

### It Happened in Colossae Too

The first-century town of Colossae was located in an agricultural area, surrounded by pastures and sheep. Though historians in the fourth and fifth centuries B.C. called Colossae a "populous and large city," gradually it had declined until, in the first century A.D., just a few years before the Apostle Paul wrote his letter to them, Strabo called Colossae a "small town." The church at Colossae was also likely small, small enough to fit in Nympha's and Philemon's homes (Colossians 4:15, Philemon 2). Whether we're talking about two different house churches or one house church that met in different places, chances are there was no megachurch in Colossae.

Like many towns today, Colossae had experienced considerable decline. And, it continued to decline after Paul wrote his letter to them until it disappeared. Colossae today is an uninhabited field, with only a few stones and other traces giving slight evidence that a once viable community was located there.

To some a declining agricultural town and small church might seem insignificant—not a place worthy of investing one's time. But this wasn't Paul's perspective. We can see this in the fact that the busy apostle set aside some of his valuable time to write a letter to them. Here was a small church in a small, declining agricultural town receiving an inspired letter from the most famous Christian in that day. Perhaps today this would be like an internationally known Christian sending a personal letter to your small-town church—not a form letter and not words quickly dashed off a computer, but a personal letter with substance and length that took some time to compose. Paul obviously highly valued this small town and church!

Some of the passages in Colossians, such as 1:15-20, will further underscore the value Paul placed on this declining small town. Why didn't Paul save these words for a larger audience? And why invest such eloquence in such a small audience? The answer: Paul viewed Colossae as an important place of ministry. He labored on its behalf just as hard as he did for the multitudes in large cities.

Are you in a declining situation? Let Paul be your inspiration. Don't let decline lull you into complacency. A respected pastor-friend who has devoted his life to small-town ministry said, "I prepare messages for 10 the same way I do for 100." That's treating small places with the dignity and respect they deserve.

Paul was also quick to commend the Colossians. In his salutation he calls them "holy and faithful." Note that he doesn't call them losers because they were in a declining small town, nor insignificant because they were in a small church. Paul's other salutations show this one to be uncharacteristic.

Beginning in 1:3 Paul heaps words of praise on this little church. He commends them for their faith and love, and for their fruitful ministry. This church may not have been located on a 40-acre campus or held several services each Sunday attended by thousands, but Paul certainly did not view it as a second-rate church!

Perhaps best of all are Paul's words for the leader in this declining town of Colossae. (By the way, can you name him? Probably not—just as the names of most small-town pastors and leaders are little known.) In 1:7 Paul affectionately refers to Epaphras as a "dear" man. He calls him a "fellow servant." There's no condescension, no viewing Epaphras as less significant because he was in a declining, small place. Paul regarded Epaphras as an equal, a *fellow* servant not a lesser servant. He further calls him a "faithful minister." Can you think of any better words that you'd like your regional minister to say about you?

Can a Christian worker in a declining small town be considered just as faithful in Christ's service as one in a bigger place? Are the words "Well done, good and faithful servant" proportionate to the size of one's ministry? Consider heaven's perspective, not the perspective of many on earth, as you contemplate your answer; that's really the only perspective that matters. The fact that one is in a declining place, and in a small church, does not cause God to deem that person as less faithful. This ought to hearten us, because Scripture indicates that God's eternal reward for each of us will be distributed on the basis of our faithfulness.

(We encourage you to do further study, determining what characteristics of Epaphras prompted Paul to commend him for being a faithful servant in a declining small town. See 1:6-7 and 4:12-13.)

### Different Kinds of Decline

*Decline* is a broad term that can be measured in countless ways. It is hard to imagine a church anywhere that does not have components of decline. The most obvious gauge that is used is numbers: decline in attendance and offerings. But couldn't decline be evident in other ways? How about a decline in enthusiasm? An increasingly unkempt church building? More and more people unwilling to serve? Creeping pessimism? A growing lack of desire for spiritual growth? Growing materialism?

On the other hand, is decline in attendance or offerings necessarily *true* decline? Statistics alone can be a simplistic way to measure decline. In some cases numerical decline might not be an indicator of real decline. While a church located in a county where the population has declined will also likely experience a decline in attendance, at the same time might the members be growing in spiritual maturity? Might they be more intentional than they used to be about creating ministry opportunities in which the gospel is shared? While the total giving of the church might be going down, might the giving per capita be going up? Might there be an increasing desire on the part of the people to serve? Might there be a growing positive spirit? Abundant evidence of healthy relationships? An increase in interest in the ministries of the church's missionaries, to the point that the congregation is praying diligently for them, communicating with them, and some even visiting them on the field? Can't all these things be happening in a church that some might consider to be in decline because its numbers are going down? Is a church like this *truly* in decline?

Certain kinds of church decline cannot be helped. Perhaps you are in a county where there used to be a farmhouse on every quarter section of ground, with a family of 12 living there, but now farmhouses are spaced several miles apart and each household has only two children. Numerical decline in your church is virtually certain. But such churches need not be in *true* decline, at least when considering the most important gauges of decline.

It might help for you to compare attendance to the changing population of the community. In one of Ron's pastorates, in a span of two years the church declined by one-fifth. But at the same time the county population declined by one-third. (This happened during the devastating farm crisis in the 1980s.) Was his church in decline?

Unfortunately one form of decline can tend to feed another. Often churches that experience a decline in attendance and offerings correspondingly experience decline in other, far more serious areas of spiritual concern. While there are some forms of decline that we can't do much about, we should give a great deal of attention to spiritual decline—a form of decline that does not necessarily follow numerical decline. Section Two provides some suggestions for leading through changes such as decline.

## An Oasis of Encouragement

Declining population, and corresponding decline in church attendance, is an example of a change that we do not initiate. It is, rather, a change that we respond to. Some changes we lead, others we lead *through*.

Properly leading the town and country church through declining times will mean making sure the church is an oasis of support and encouragement. Farmers don't need the church telling them how they could have done things differently to avoid losing their farms. They need a listening ear, a shoulder to cry on. They need a church family that will stand by them in crisis, that will build them up when they are feeling beaten down. Leaders need to set the tone for this.

While you are building others up, take care to guard your own mental and emotional well-being. Pessimism is contagious. While agrarians struggle with self-image because of failures on the farm, the pastor and other church leaders may similarly suffer because of decline in the church. It can help farmers and church leaders alike if they recognize that the forces behind much decline are far bigger than any one farmer or pastor can stave off.

The greatest challenge facing many small-town churches is to avoid slipping into a survival, or even a maintenance, mentality. A vicious cycle can develop: The church desperately needs new people to keep from dying. To get new people, the church needs to launch new ministries and update its facility. But how can the church with declining attendance do these things? And why do them anyway, if the church is going to die in a few years?

One member of a rural church consistently said at church meetings, "Why should we do such and such? The church will be closed in five years." Obviously such a mentality will paralyze a church. The pastor went to the church member privately and said, "Listen, if the church is going to close in five years, why waste money and effort now? Let's close it this week." That member never made another negative public comment again. Today that church's facility has been upgraded and its membership is larger and younger.

We can counter a survival mentality in our churches by encouraging the people to take risks for God. By creatively envisioning ways our church can move forward. By continually assessing and nurturing our church's health. By initiating change that is needed. By making sure that our church is an oasis of encouragement. And by implementing the steps for change discussed in Section Two—doable even in declining contexts.

Before embarking on the steps necessary to bring about change in declining situations, and indeed all the situations mentioned in these early chapters, it is crucial that we first accurately identify the changes that are needed. Chapter six will help you do that. However, let's first look at a few more important changes that have been happening in town and country areas.

CHAPTER FOUR

# A Disappearing Act

## *The change: Fading of the middle class, emergence of the new rural poor and rural rich*

**TOM PARKER STOOD ON THE 115-YEAR-OLD FRONT STEPS** of the Smithville Community Church and looked down Main Street. He had been a leader at the church for 35 years and attended there all his life. As he looked down the street he saw the ghosts of the village's past. An elementary school built during the early 1960s was now vacant, its roof sagging and windows broken. Only the concrete platform of the railroad station remained, the tracks having been taken out in the '80s. The old bank was now a tavern, the grocery store sat empty, and the hardware store now housed a seasonal second-hand and antique shop. Smithville looked like a ghost town, except for one thing: nearly all of the houses were still occupied.

Next door to the church was the parsonage. It looked about the same as it always had. But beyond it, in the Warners' old house, there were new residents. A rusty pickup and partially disassembled motorcycle sat in the front yard, amidst a scattering of kids' toys. Tom had seen a woman there, and several kids, and three different men seemed to come and go. He didn't know their names.

As Tom looked on down the street, he could recall the names of folks who had lived in every house 30 years ago, what they had done for a living, and what volunteer positions each had filled at the annual town festival. Now he was surrounded by all these new folks and he didn't know them, and he wasn't sure he wanted to. When they did visit church they always seemed to ask for money, if not the first Sunday at least by the third. Tom shook his head sadly. These were a different kind of folks, these new residents of Smithville.

Tom got in his car and started to drive the 12 miles to his home in the county seat, where he and Velma had moved after he had retired. A couple of miles out of Smithville he passed a new home being built on the highway. It had beautiful brick with arched windows and a three-car garage. Tom had heard that some fellow from the city was building it. Supposedly it was the same man who had been buying up hundreds of acres at farm auctions. As he drove past Tom wondered, *Why does anyone need a house that big? Will the family attend the Smithville Community Church?*

Looking over Tom Parker's shoulder, you can see another of the big changes taking place in rural places: the emergence of a new rural poor and a new rural rich. At the same time, it seems the middle class in many rural areas is disappearing. These changes are more apparent in some areas than others and take different shapes in different places.

## The New Rural Poor

The new rural poor is a group distinct from the traditional poor of rural areas. Traditionally, the poor in rural areas have owned enough land to graze a few animals and raise a garden, and they owned their own homes, although these homes may have been very modest. The poorer members of a community were lifelong residents and as such they had friends from childhood and relatives in the community who helped them when they needed assistance.

Additionally, the traditional rural poor received strong support from the community and were valued as community members, not only for their longevity but because they had some special skill or role that benefited the community, like being good at roofing or handling livestock. Because they had valued skills, they had some modest earning capacity. They might never rise above poverty level but they were generally self-sufficient. In short, they viewed themselves and were viewed by the community as contributing members. The same was true of their relationship to the church. They would give to the church what little they could, even if it was just a few dollars, or their labor, or produce from their garden. These traditional rural poor have been a part of the town and country scene for generations.

In recent years a new kind of rural poor has burst onto the scene. These new folks are very different from the traditional poor of rural communities, and many of them are new to rural places entirely. As mentioned in the chapter on depopulation, there are fewer and fewer farmers and ranchers, meaning there is less need for housing for agrarians. Correspondingly, many businesses in nearby villages have shut down. This leaves thousands of rural villages scattered across the country that are full of empty houses no one wants to buy, which has greatly reduced their value. So, the rural landlords buy these houses and rent them for low rates, and often don't pay much attention to them otherwise. With absentee or inattentive landlords, and business districts full of abandoned buildings, these villages have come to exhibit problems similar to those of some blighted urban areas. Into these houses are moving low-income occupants, some of them speaking languages other than English, many coming from the cities to find lower rents, safer neighborhoods, and—they are hoping—an untapped source of generosity.

The new rural poor rarely own their own homes or any land. They instead rent on short-term lease contracts, sometimes just on a verbal agreement. These new residents frequently move on, often in as little as a year's time. They may come from families that have been dysfunctional for generations and therefore lack much family support. Because they are new to the community and are often alien to the rural culture, they also lack community support and frequently aren't even noticed, although in many cases they begin to outnumber the traditional residents of the community. Because they often lack marketable skills, they are more entitlement-oriented and dependent on government transfer payments. They tend to come to church expecting to be a supported client rather than a contributing member.

The chart below shows the differences at a glance between these two groups of rural poor.

## RURAL POOR, THEN AND NOW

| Characteristic | Traditional Rural Poor | New Rural Poor |
|---|---|---|
| Property | Own small acreage | Own no land |
| Housing | Own | Rent |
| Tenure | Lifelong | 12-18 months |
| Family support | Strong | Very little |
| Community support | Strong/highly valued | Weak/not valued |
| Economics | Self-sufficient | Entitlement dependent |
| Capacity to earn | At least somewhat skilled | Unskilled |
| View of church | A place to be a contributing member/friend | A place to be a supported client |

The new rural poor bring a real challenge to the town and country church. The church may already be trying to conserve resources due to declining numbers as long-time members die or move away. When the church leadership looks out on the sea of need in their own backyard, they may feel overwhelmed by what they see.

### The New Rural Rich

You might recall, when looking over Tom Parker's shoulder, that not everything he saw was poverty. At the other end of the spectrum are the rural rich. Some of the rich are increasingly bigger farmers, many of whom inherited much of their land. Some are "secret rich" people who live like everyone else, or at least appear to, but have lots of money. These are the more traditional rural rich.

However, there is another class of wealthy people: the new rural rich. In recent years, entertainment and sports stars have purchased farms, ranches, and woodlands to have as country estates. Some wealthy city people, many of them professionals who are willing to commute up to 90 minutes to work, are increasingly being motivated to move out into rural areas—perhaps because they are looking for a more sprawling environment in which to live and enjoy their "toys." Some are moving to the country because they are seeking isolation. (Ecclesiastes 5:11 speaks of how wealthy people tend to seek isolation because increased wealth brings new "friends" that continually hound them.) Some are not imports but local people who have become newly rich because a newfound source of wealth has emerged in the area: Wal-Mart headquartering in northwest Arkansas, new tourist attractions putting outsiders' money into local pockets, an auto manufacturer building a new plant and hiring local people. The new rural rich also comprise retirees with plentiful cash who have been moving to small towns at an unprecedented rate, seeking to enjoy the tranquility and simplicity that they perceive is found in rural places.

Large corporate farms, foreign investors, and agribusiness companies are currently buying up millions of acres. The owners and/or managers of these large holdings are also an emerging component of the new rural rich.

## Land of Opportunity

Like the new rural poor, the new rural rich bring a huge challenge to the town and country church. These may be some of the most unreached people in the country. This is true in part because many of them are fiercely private due to their wary suspicions of all the new "friends" that seem to accompany their wealth. Some are not receptive to overtures from Christians because acquiring and enjoying wealth is a higher priority to them than an active faith. (According to Matthew 19:23 it is more difficult for the rich to enter the kingdom of heaven.) It is also difficult to attract the rural rich because they are often reluctant to mix with "common country folk," including the rural poor.

Rural poor and rural rich have come to town and country areas in great numbers. We must see both groups as people whom Jesus wants to love through us. This is one of the changes that must come to town and country churches if they are to be faithful to the Great Commission (Matthew 28:19-20).

Thus far we have addressed some considerable changes that have come to town and country areas: Repopulation. Depopulation. The new poor and new rich. But we have yet to discuss what we believe is the most significant change of all—the change that ought to be the greatest focus of the church today in rural places. The next chapter addresses that change.

CHAPTER FIVE

# A Crisis in Rural Communities

## *The change: Less "wholesome country living"*

**RON'S EARLY YEARS WERE SPENT ON A FARM**. Then his family moved to the city. Nearly 20 years later when Ron moved back to the country, he found that things had changed in lots of ways, some more obvious than others. Out in the fields farmers are no longer using three-bottom plows pulled by Massey Ferguson tractors that seem scarcely bigger than the riding lawn mowers of today. Now he hardly ever sees plowing being done. In fact, he notes that much of the make-up of many town and country areas is no longer heavily influenced by agriculture. He sees that the young don't dress like farm kids. He sees farmers' wives and even some farmers going off to Big Town to work an eight-to-five job. He sees new subdivisions in the cornfields. He sees lots of change.

However, one change that Ron observes, not only in towns where he has lived but also in his travels that have frequently criss-crossed the United States and Canada, is not as visibly evident when driving through a rural area. Though not as visible, this is the most significant change this book addresses. This major change is the erosion of spiritual values and the accompanying decline in morality. A recent article in *The New York Times* succinctly explains what is happening.[3] Many others have documented this change as well. Let's consider the evidence.

---

[3]Timothy Egan, "Pastoral Poverty: The Seeds of Decline," *The New York Times*, December 8, 2002.

## Evidences of a Spiritual Crisis

Many types of crime are more likely now to happen in town and country areas than previously. Whereas people in rural places used to only lock their cars in July (to keep friends from filling them with zucchini from their gardens!), now it is advisable in many places to lock the doors year around. The number of rural property crimes, like residential burglaries, has risen substantially. Towns of 10,000-25,000 have become the most likely places to experience bank robberies.

Drugs have become an increasing scourge in rural areas. Cheap labs make methamphetamine ("meth" or "speed") from anhydrous ammonia fertilizer, which is found on nearly every farm. These labs abound in the country, where they are easily hidden from law enforcement authorities. The White House calls this the fastest-growing drug threat in America. Users of meth tend to be white and rural. Drug lab seizures in some Midwestern states are skyrocketing at a more than tenfold increase in just a few years' time. In a recent year, there were 300 times more meth lab seizures in Iowa than in New York and New Jersey combined. In Wyoming, officials estimate that 1 out of 100 people needs treatment for meth addiction.

Meth causes major problems in rural communities. Users tend to be erratic, violent, and, in some cases, borderline psychotic. Users lose their jobs, steal, batter their spouses and loved ones, abandon their families, and war among one another .

"Meth seems to be everywhere in Nebraska right now," Mr. Curtis of the Nebraska Crime Commission recently said, "with poor white kids making meth out of their cars." Just a short time ago when Ron was visiting a small town in Nebraska, a pastor there told him meth production was the primary source of income in his county. We hope he was exaggerating.

Alcohol use among rural young people has skyrocketed in recent years to nearly three times that of their city counterparts. Depression, suicide, and illicit sex are also more prevalent among rural young people.

The family, once a mainstay of the rural community, is experiencing the same kind of disintegration that is taking place in urban areas. For instance, the number of single-mother families in nonmetropolitan communities has been increasing at a faster rate than in metropolitan areas.

The rate of serious crime in Nebraska, Kansas, Oklahoma, and Utah is as much as 50 percent higher than the state of New York, according to F.B.I. reports. Some sparsely populated areas have higher murder rates than New York City, straining small-town police budgets to the point that many are begging the federal government for help. In the last decade, drug-related homicides fell by 50 percent in urban areas, but tripled in the countryside.

Several years ago, after Ron and his wife Roxy had together spoken at a Bible college missions conference, one of the missions professors who specializes in inner-city ministry came to the platform and said to them, "If I didn't know that you were talking about rural communities, I would have thought you were talking about inner cities." Then he made this observation: "I've come to realize that there are a lot of similarities between inner-city and rural ministry. I used to view locales on a spectrum: from inner city, to suburban, to rural—thinking that the further you live out from the inner city, the more different your environment is. Now I realize that inner cities and rural areas have many similarities and that really it's the suburbs that are different." This comment could apply to a number of characteristics of inner cities and rural places, but certainly none as significant as the spiritual changes being described in this chapter.

This decline in spiritual vitality is certainly not true of every small town. There are many exceptions. However, most readers are probably nodding your heads, reluctantly affirming that we are describing your beloved community.

What we have been relating is, at its core, a spiritual crisis. Historically, town and country communities have been the spiritual bedrock of North America, places with a fairly steady and consistent moral base and values. But this is fast eroding. Because this change is a spiritual crisis, we rank it as being the most significant. While the other changes we have highlighted have spiritual dimensions, this change most directly has eternal ramifications.

### Addressing the Crisis

If any progress is going to be made in solving this spiritual crisis, the first step is to acknowledge that it exists. Those of us who live and serve in town and country places cannot have our heads in the sand, ignoring the reality that is surrounding us. We must be wary of concluding, "This isn't happening here." We must come to grips with the fact that "wholesome country living" no longer describes the lifestyle of many rural communities. Norman Rockwell paintings and old *Andy Griffith* episodes about life in Mayberry no longer accurately depict life in many town and country settings.

A second step in solving this crisis is to ask hard questions about its causes, which are likely many. For instance, it is probably no coincidence that spiritual decline is coinciding with the recent influx of newcomers moving to the country, as we addressed in chapter two, and the emergence of the new rural poor and rich, as we addressed in chapter four. However, we must be careful not to paint too broad a stroke with this conclusion. It would be simplistic for us to place the blame for all these changes at the feet of a few transplants.

Certainly the media blanketing the country through satellite and cable television have created more of a level playing field when it comes to the spreading of sin. It used to be that certain sins hadn't found their way to remote areas, but this is no longer so.

As automation has reduced the need for young people to do chores, boredom in isolated areas has been on the increase and gotten many in trouble. Idle hands are indeed the devil's workshop. Two besetting sins of town and country areas, substance abuse (particularly alcohol and meth) and illicit sex, are readily available in remote places. One needn't travel a lot of miles or spend a lot of money to get either.

Because these are spiritual issues, we must take a hard look at whether our churches are in some way contributing to the problem, directly or indirectly, consciously or unconsciously. It can be sobering and difficult for the church to acknowledge and accept its share of responsibility. One way the church might accept responsibility is the subject of this book: the importance of leading through the change that is happening around us.

What happens when a traditional farm church continues to act as a farm church though it is no longer in a community that is predominantly made up of farmers? That church is not likely to positively affect newcomers or their spiritual values. This may lead to an erosion of their values, which may in turn affect other long-term residents in the community.

What happens when a church's approach to ministry hasn't adapted in such a way that it connects with the upcoming generation? If the church's influence among teens is anemic at best, we shouldn't be surprised to find abundant evidence of increasing spiritual decline in young people.

What happens when the majority of people in a church have slowly, over many years, grown spiritually stagnant, with little evidence of change (i.e., growth) in their lives? Can we expect these folks to have a positive impact on their communities?

Think about it from the positive side. What happens when lives are transformed in a town or country context, a place where everyone knows about it and can see it unfolding? What happens when the town drunk repents, puts his faith in Christ, and lives a changed life? What happens when a well-known family steps into the baptismal waters together? What happens when a vibrant church in town is a frequent topic of conversation?

The spiritual crisis described in this chapter, and the hope for renewal and its accompanying impact, is a major impetus behind this book. It is also a major focus of Section Two, which will help guide you through the change process, starting with how to carefully assess and understand the changes that need to be implemented in your church. Chapter six specifically addresses diagnosing our situations; without doing that, we may very well work toward initiating the wrong kinds of changes.

## section two

# Steps for Leading Your Town or Country Church Through Change

**WE NOW TURN TO SOME PRACTICAL TIPS**, more of a how-to section. Section One related changes that are happening but said only a little about what might be done about those changes. Our intention in this section is to offer more practical, hands-on advice.

This section not only revisits some of the challenging changes described in Section One, it also examines other kinds of changes that are frequently called for in town and country churches. We want to wed these changes with a process for change. In other words, we want to make sure the rubber is going to meet the road, that you're able to glean from this book a clear sense of how you might slowly and surely lead your church through change.

We anticipate that parts of Section One will soon become dated. Such is the nature of change today, even in town and country areas. Section Two, we believe, will be more timeless.

Section One was more passive. It spoke, for the most part, of changes in town and country areas that we have not initiated, changes that are not of our doing. Section Two is more proactive about change. We want to suggest a process that will help you *lead* through change, including steps that will help you bring change to your town or country context.

Section One may have contained chapters that do not apply to your ministry context. We gave you permission to skip those chapters. That permission is now rescinded for the chapters that follow! Our hope is that you will read every one of them.

We begin with a chapter that will help you be discerning about the changes that are happening around you, in how you assess these changes, and how your church might respond in concert with its changing environment. When concluding that there is a desperate need for change, it is easy to make the wrong changes or go about the changes in the wrong way. We hope the following chapters will help you avoid some of these pitfalls.

## Chapter Six

# Seeing the Need

**CHARLIE OPENED HIS CLOSET DOOR** to choose a shirt for the day. He took one out, slipped it on, and started to button it up. It was tight. He hung it back in the closet, concluding he must have gained a bit of weight over the weekend. He chose another, one he had bought after the Christmas holidays. If there was a time of the year when Charlie filled out a shirt, it was then. This shirt hung a little baggy on him. He put it back in the closet. He took out the next one, then put it right back after seeing the big brown splotch where he had spilled wood stain.

Ah, there was one of his favorites, a long-sleeved wool shirt with a quilted lining. He remembered how warm and comfortable it was last winter when he was shoveling snow. But before he finished buttoning it, Charlie realized it was much too warm now that spring had come. Charlie took yet another shirt from the closet. It had a frayed collar, a torn pocket, and was missing a button.

He returned that shirt to the closet and took out the last remaining one. This was his favorite. It fit well, was comfortable, and was still in pretty good shape. But Charlie returned it to his closet. Every time he tried to wear that shirt his wife and daughters complained about how out-of-style it was and refused to be seen in public with him.

Charlie needs a change of wardrobe—for the same reasons that some churches need to make changes:

- Like the first two shirts, the congregation or community may be growing or shrinking, and something about the current program, personnel, or facilities no longer fits.
- Like the stained shirt, a catastrophic event can force a change no one intended.

- Like the wool shirt, something that worked well earlier no longer works due to changed conditions.

- Like the old shirt, sometimes structures, programs, and even people just wear out.

- Like Charlie's favorite shirt, a program or ministry that may have nothing wrong with it is simply not well received or looked upon favorably, perhaps perceived as outdated.

For Charlie, it wasn't hard to see the need for a wardrobe change. Unfortunately, it is not always quite as easy to see the need for change in the church.

## How to See the Need

Seeing the need for change seems to continually be a challenge for those who are Christ's disciples, from the first century to today. In John 4:35, as a whole town of Samaritans streamed out to see Jesus, He asked His disciples, "Do you not say, 'Four months more and then the harvest?' I tell you, open your eyes and look at the fields! They are ripe for harvest." Here was an entire town of "unchurched" folks of a different ethnic background. Change in thinking and strategy was desperately needed to reach them, but the disciples didn't see the need.

How does one begin to see the need for change? Some needs are obvious: a building lies in ruins—either because of fire or storm, a key leader dies, the town's major employer shuts down. These kinds of changes smack a congregation right in the face and the congregation simply must respond. The vast majority of needed changes, however, are neither so obvious nor so unavoidable. Church leaders must be on the lookout for the need for less obvious changes by keeping a close eye on the congregation and community.

In metropolitan areas, market research firms and government agencies continually seek information that will inform of the need for change. Churches as well as businesses can access this information. But few marketing firms exist in rural places, so churches there will have to ask questions and find answers for themselves.

Let's start with the congregation. Keeping records of such things as attendance and offerings, including the attendance of classes and other gatherings that meet regularly, will help you spot trends and patterns, which in turn will help you plan for the future. At least once a year the leadership should look at each household in the church, noting such things as their ages, places of employment, and number of children. By comparing this information with that of previous years, you can discern if the average age of the congregation is shifting, what's happening with the children, whether the employment base is changing, and other things. These changes have a way of sneaking up on congregations, even small-town congregations, unless there are intentional steps taken to identify them. One reason many churches fail to make the changes they should is because changes around them happen so gradually that they aren't noticed.

This can especially be true with changes in the church's demographic make-up. Consider the experience of one rural church. In one decade the employment base of the community changed from being 95 percent agricultural to less than 20 percent. What kinds of changes might need to be made in the church to coincide with this change in the community? It could be that seasonal activities which have for years been oriented to agriculture need to change. Perhaps leaders should watch for emerging cultural tensions between agrarians and cosmopolitans (see chapter two for some help).

In that same period the number of wives who worked outside the home or farm increased ten-fold. What kinds of changes might this bring to the church? Perhaps a large pool of women can no longer be counted on to staff children's programs or attend daytime Bible studies. It might signal the need for changing to an evening Vacation Bible School.

That same church was blessed with a number of babies born in a two-year period. This signaled the immediate need for changes in the nursery. It also signaled a need to begin thinking about revamping children's and youth programs.

Suppose that, instead of many babies being born, many heads are graying in the congregation? This might signal a need for more focus on seniors' ministry. Suppose the average age in the community is not changing but the average age of church attenders is going up? This indicates that the church needs to take a look at what might be done to reach younger people.

Along with monitoring the congregation, it is just as important to monitor the community and discern whether changes there might affect the church. Some changes in the community will be obvious, like the closing of a mine or the opening of a new factory, but most changes will be more subtle and take place gradually over months or years. Watch for changes in the community's size, people's occupations, and commuting distances. Any of these can be signals that the church needs to change the ways it is reaching out to the community.

Besides being a careful observer, look at data that others have gathered. Every 10 years, in order to plan and implement needed changes, the federal government conducts a census. The census information provides answers for these five questions church leaders should ask: How many people live here? How old are they? What is their ethnicity? What is their occupation? What is their income?

But often census data aren't specific or informative enough because they don't zero in on a particular small town. You can glean more information on how your community is changing by asking the school superintendent, local law enforcement officials, and a real estate agent. For instance, the school superintendent will know how many children are in each grade and how this differs from last year. A decline in the number of elementary children indicates an aging population, while an increase suggests that young couples are moving into town. The superintendent will know what percentage of the student population qualifies for government lunch subsides. This number will be an indication of how many families are living in poverty. Comparing this number with previous years will tell you if the town's economy is improving or declining. The school superintendent can tell you the percentage of students for whom English is not a first language. If this number is above 10 percent and is increasing, the church should consider a ministry for non-English-speaking households.

The town's police officer or county sheriff has another view of life in the community. From that person you can learn about the problems the youth in the community are facing, the rates of domestic violence, the types and frequency of drug use, and other indicators that reveal the spiritual needs of the community. The local law enforcement officer is also aware of problems and issues that are not classified as criminal, such as the number of latchkey kids or homeless persons. These may suggest opportunities for ministry.

The local real estate agent (many towns have only one or two) knows a great deal about how the community is changing. That person can tell you if new residents are looking for five-acre mini-ranches, new homes on the edge of town, older homes with "character," or income-indexed apartments. The agent can tell you if the rate of turnover in the area is increasing or decreasing and why. She or he can also tell you if a number of homes are coming on the market because people are leaving the area, and if homes and lots are being sold to outsiders. A good agent will quickly pick up on whether your community is becoming a bedroom community for commuters, a retirement destination, or a little piece of urban slum out in the country. Developing a good working relationship with the local realtor will not only help you gain information about change in your community, it may also get you referrals to new families looking for a church.

There are many other people who may have their own unique insights into community change: public health workers, university extension representatives, workers who hook up newcomers' utilities services, or other people in the church or community who are paying attention to what is going on around them.

For Ron, the utilities man who oversaw the hooking up of electric meters was a godsend. He once told Ron that in the past three months he had hooked up about a dozen meters for newcomers in their town of 500. Ron was shocked. He passed the news on to the evangelism committee. They responded with disbelief, until further investigation produced real names. The committee developed a plan for welcoming newcomers to town and befriending them. A number of them became a part of the church.

We encourage you to get out in the community and talk to people and, more important, listen to them. They will help you see the needs for changes. As church leaders monitor changes around them, it is possible that they will discover community changes that are not reflected in the congregation.

Additional reasons exist for initiating change besides responding to changes happening around us, either within or outside the church. Sometimes a church needs a shot in the arm. Or sometimes a church has a weakness that needs to be shored up. Or, as with one of Charlie's shirts, sometimes things just wear out or lose their effectiveness.

### Mini-Changes

After seeing the need for change, the next issue that must be wrestled with is the process of change. Should change in town and country areas normally be large or incremental? Should most changes happen quickly? If we say yes to either or both questions just asked, we might conclude that leading change in town and country areas is only for the smart, the brave, the skilled, or hard-charging people with high energy.

In most cases, changes in town and country churches should be *evolutionary* rather than *revolutionary*.[4] With few exceptions, we strongly

---

[4]This terminology comes from John Macdonald, *Calling a Halt to Mindless Change* (New York: The American Management Association International, 1998).

suggest that the chosen course of action should be mini-changes. Numerous little changes add up to big change over time. This means that leading the town and country church through change calls for patience and perseverance.

Given the historical and cultural context, mini-changes are generally preferred in town and country churches. In rural areas change has tended to come more slowly and with some reluctance. In such a context, revolutionary change may cause more harm than good, even when the change itself is successfully implemented.

The space shuttle is always moved from the hanger to the launch pad at a painfully slow speed. This is not because technicians don't have the know-how or ability to move it faster but because there is so much more potential for harm to the shuttle if they are in too much of a hurry. Will a faster pace preclude a successful launch? No. But there is so much more potential for harm.

So it is in the town and country church when we try to move change along too quickly. Hurt feelings might be aroused because someone's good idea from a few years back is being thrown out instead of tweaked. Relationships might be strained. A segment of the church might either decide to leave or move to the sidelines, neither of which can be afforded in a small church. A tight-lipped, grim minority might be created, people with considerable anger just below the surface, a time bomb waiting to explode.

Just as choosing the appropriate pace for change avoids potential harm, employing incremental change elevates the *process*. Process is as important as the end result. Process is ministry. Ministry doesn't begin after the change is completed; ideally ministry will happen during the process of change. Both route and destination hold great promise. There is much that can be gained along the way. We must resist thinking that gain will only begin after we've arrived. Thus we strongly emphasize the importance of the phrase "leading *through* change"—*through* is a process word.

For instance, perhaps change is needed in worship style, Before the change itself is made, you can teach your congregation theology related to worship. You can teach your congregation the importance of deferring to one another. You can teach your congregation how to properly work through differences. You can instill a philosophy of inter-generational ministry that encourages an openness to various worship styles. So much can be missed if you rush to make a change in worship style without considering the importance of the process in getting there.

The same can be true with regard to starting a ministry for the new rural poor. There are opportunities for learning and experimenting before the actual changes are made. For example, consider familiarizing yourself with a few books on inner-city ministry, the culture of which has a striking resemblance to the new rural poor. Through preaching, cultivate the right kind of attitude in your congregation's hearts toward the new rural poor. Work toward instilling in them the willingness to minister unconditionally to those who may not reciprocate in any way. The process could be what God uses to give people in your church the passion needed to reach the poor for Christ. To abort the process and rush into launching a program could result in people being reluctant to minister, or ministering with minimal effectiveness, or ministering out of a sense of duty instead of with hearts of love.

Before launching a ministry that targets newcomers who have moved into town, much can be gained by helping your congregation understand its own culture in contrast to the culture of those who are moving in. As we said in chapter two, here is a chance to teach your congregation "Cultural Anthropology 101." For years a disproportionately large number of rural people have gone to other cultures to serve as missionaries, with those who remain at home strongly supporting them. Now the mission field is coming to them as other cultures move into rural areas. This provides an unprecedented opportunity for rural people to be missionaries right in their own community! What is God's heart for these people? How would He say we should reach them? What attitudes need to be adopted or avoided? What approaches to ministry should change? What things that we hold dear need to be let go of for the sake of the gospel? How can we differentiate between the timeless and the temporary? What is the proper way for our congregation to come to an agreement on what changes need to be made?

The process of change is vitally important. It must not be shortchanged.

### Choosing the Change

After seeing the need for change and considering the importance of the process, the next issue is how to choose from the many options. There are seemingly endless numbers of changes a church could make, and leaders are often bombarded from all directions with ideas. Books and magazines come out every week suggesting new ways of doing things.

Seminars espousing ideas for change abound. Folks in the congregation continually come up with all kinds of ideas for change. Visits to other congregations will trigger still more ideas for possible changes.

A church could, for example, install a skateboard park in the back parking lot or start a Bible study for professional dogsled racers. These are just two among the unlimited number of changes a church *could* make (and either of which, in the right context, *may* be the right change to make). The important task for leading a particular church through change is to know which changes that church *should* make. Let's look at how to decide which changes to lead.

When considering change, it is important to correctly assess our situation or we will choose the wrong change. We may think we need to change our church's worship style simply because we hear how others are worshiping elsewhere; however, the reality may be that our present style is appropriate for our particular context. Or we may be correct in assessing that a change of worship style is indeed needed, but then opt for the wrong style.

We may think we need to put more emphasis on youth ministry ("They're the future of our church!"), when the demographics tell us the community is made up of predominately retired people. The "future of the church" then is 60-year-olds who are nearing retirement age, and changes that are made should have them in mind.

We may hear or observe how a particular change is making a difference in other churches and be tempted to import that into our church— only to find out it was the wrong thing to do. For example: moving to a seeker service format. While success stories abound of churches that have done so, it is likely that this would be a difficult change in most small-town churches. For example, seeker services require a substantial pool of unbelievers to draw from, and the anonymity that most seekers prefer is nearly impossible to maintain in town and country areas!

When considering change, it is crucial that we be discerning. In order to be a good change for a rural church to make, that change should meet these four criteria: it must be (1) strongly needed, (2) theologically correct, (3) culturally appropriate, and (4) doable. Let's consider each of these.

First, there must be clear evidence of need. Often changes come about mindlessly without a clear need established. A common way that this occurs is when folks hear about something that is happening elsewhere and immediately conclude it should happen where they are. It could be that this change was appropriate somewhere else; it truly is meeting a need there. But that doesn't mean the need is present where you are. Even if the need is present, it may not be a compelling need. Further, it doesn't mean that the change will work well in your church.

For example, in many suburban communities the common wisdom is that the first church staff member that should be added is a youth worker. But in a rural community with few youth and a lot of seniors, this would not likely be a good change. A better change might be to add a staff member who works with seniors. Making a change just because other churches are doing it, without confirming that your church or community needs such a change, is a waste of resources and effort.

Second, there must be theological correctness. In Acts 15 the church was facing a proposed change—a big one. The change was welcoming Gentiles (who were different both culturally and ethnically) into the church. More than welcoming them into the local church, at stake was nothing less than the question of who can be a Christian. Fortunately, the first-century leaders were perceptive. They saw that the question was first and foremost a theological issue and, therefore, must be answered accordingly. The Jerusalem conference convened to discuss theology.

Churches that are working toward change often make one of two mistakes: either they fail to think about the theological implications of the change or they find theological arguments for or against (usually against) the change that do not really apply. Often the motive for skirting theology is that they simply want to adopt an innovation from another church because they like it or "it works." Or they are opposed to it simply because they don't like it or are slow to accept change. Failing to assess whether there are underlying theological issues that should be addressed is irresponsible leadership and can be spiritually dangerous. A caution: Sometimes in the process of deciding the theological correctness of a change, people strain Scripture to support one side or the other. Leaders should consider every change carefully and thoughtfully in light of an accurate interpretation of Scripture to ensure that it is theologically correct.

The third criterion is cultural appropriateness. Missionaries working in foreign countries are careful to ensure that the ways they present the gospel and "do church" will not needlessly conflict with the local culture. Pastors working in North America often assume that there is one homogenous culture here and that what works somewhere will work everywhere. This is not true.

Consider music. Missionary ethnomusicologists study the musical forms of the culture in order to write worship music in the local forms, but in North America we are prone to assume that all church music everywhere should sound the same and the methods of leading worship should be the same. Many urban and suburban churches are now using "worship teams" and "praise bands" with multiple singers, electronic instrumentation, and the words to songs projected on a screen. (Like many trends, this trend may well change.) Such "contemporary worship music" has a form of its own. Because it is so common, many rural churches assume changing to this musical form is the right thing to do. And, it may be—or it may not. In many rural communities the culturally appropriate musical form may be Southern gospel or bluegrass. One recently planted small-town church that had used a contemporary format since the church's beginnings purchased a piano and large-print hymnals when it realized that most of the unchurched people in town were senior citizens with traditional church backgrounds. Doing so was a culturally appropriate change for that church.

Cultural sensitivity includes being aware of seasonal time demands on farmers and ranchers, of the high school athletic schedule, and of the timing of special community events. Integrating a change on the church calendar with the rhythms of community life will help ensure the success of the change.

A change may meet these first three criteria with flying colors and yet simply not be doable. Your church may want to start a preschool but your building may not be up to code for that use or you don't have a qualified teacher. You might benefit from adding on a multi-purpose room, but your church is landlocked. If you try to force a change that isn't doable, and in the process are straining people and resources to the breaking point, that change isn't likely Spirit-driven. We believe that when God is in a change, He will open the doors.

When you have identified a general need for change in your church, either in response to changes in the community or because you sense the church would benefit from the infusion of change, then you would do well to commit yourself to a carefully chosen process, realizing that the process could be as important as the change itself. Then you are ready to begin to look at all the possibilities. Doing so, you must first consider specific ministry needs, theological correctness, cultural appropriateness, and whether it is doable.

We suspect that many of you, at this point, are overwhelmed with the numbers of changes that you see as necessary for your church. Before you begin the process of leading your congregation through change, we would like to help make your situation less daunting and more manageable. That's what the next chapter is all about.

## CHAPTER SEVEN

# Four Kinds of Change

**AFTER BEING IN YOUR PLACE OF MINISTRY** for some time, it is quite possible that you have become overwhelmed by the magnitude of changes that are needed in your town or country church—perhaps both the great number of changes that are needed as well as the large scope of some of the changes. Having visited many hundreds of town and country churches through the years, we have seen first hand that the amount of change that is needed in some situations can be so enormous that it is hard to know where to start, or even muster up the courage to start. We'd like to offer some help and encouragement.

For more than 15 years now, Ron has overseen pastors who are serving town and country churches. Through the years he has often encouraged pastors to consider four areas of change and to simultaneously be working to bring small changes in all of these areas: personal, ministry, infrastructure, and facility. If these pastors will, over time, be incrementally working toward change in these four areas, it is virtually guaranteed that the result will be nothing short of *big* change, though no single change in itself may be all that big. And most important, if a thoughtful, evolutionary approach toward change is taken (see chapter nine), the changes will go smoothly and be welcomed by most or all of the congregation.

## Personal Change

When we consider change, the first place we need to look is at our personal lives. We can't expect to be innovative at church but not be innovative at home. Let's put it another way: It is hard to imagine pastors or other church leaders being successful at leading change in the church while not exhibiting clear evidence of change in their lives.

Why is it important that there be change happening in our personal lives? There are several reasons. One is that if we make the church our sole focus of innovation, putting all our creative energies there, we will likely be discouraged. We may find that the congregation simply doesn't want to change, or they want to change in a different way, or at a different pace. This will eat at us a lot less if there is innovation happening in our personal and family lives. Then, when innovation isn't happening as we think it should at church, we won't be nearly as frustrated.

Many facets of life are open to innovation. For instance, try a new prayer pattern or interject music into your quiet times with God. Expand your reading to include unfamiliar topics or a different genre of literature. Introduce your family to a new sport or hobby. (This is doubly important in a remote place. The alternative may be to sit on lawn chairs and listen to rust grow on hubcaps!) Take a vacation to a place you have never been before. If you are a newcomer, work hard at adapting to the culture of your new community. If we as leaders don't adapt, how can we expect our congregation to adapt to the culture that is being introduced by newcomers who are moving in around them?

In most of these areas just mentioned we do not necessarily *have* to be innovative. The exception to this is cultural innovation, which is essential (see 1 Corinthians 9:19-23). However, if we're not innovative in our personal lives, aren't we failing to lead by example? If we put all of our "change eggs" in the church basket, aren't we setting ourselves up for frustration and disappointment when change doesn't happen as quickly as we'd like?

Try this exercise: Put this book down for a few minutes, take a sheet of paper, and try to come up with at least 20 ways that you could bring change into your personal life.

### Ministry Change

For hundreds of years, the primary tool of the grain farmer was the moldboard plow. Used each spring to cut through the vegetation and turn over the soil before planting, the plow was synonymous with farming. But one would be hard pressed to find a plow among today's farmers. Conservation tillage methods and chemical technology have made the plow virtually unnecessary, and a waste of time and money. Such changes also come to the ministries of town and country churches. Just as plowing served a need that no longer exists, so many churches continue ministries targeting needs that no longer exist.

To start on the path of making ministry changes, we encourage you to list every ministry of your church: every group that meets, every class that's offered, every service performed. Now go back through your list and ask whom each ministers to and why it is needed. Some of your church's ministries will no doubt still be vital, some will likely be marginal, and some may be benefiting few if anyone.

Before ministries are scrapped, try brainstorming about some ministries your church and/or community needs but doesn't have. Is there an age, social, or ethnic group in your community that the church isn't reaching? Is there a need for a men's ministry, a moms' group, some type of support or recovery group, a daycare or an after-school program? List all the ministry needs you can think of in the church and community.

Because people often equate their value and usefulness in the Kingdom with the particular ministry in which they work, doing away with that ministry may seriously threaten their sense of worth. Therefore, you would do well to ask if it is possible to beat a plowshare into a sword—or coffee pot, or jungle gym. In other words, can one of the ministries that has become obsolete be transformed into a ministry that is now needed, without completely dismantling the old one? If it can, you accomplish the creation of a ministry you really need without threatening or offending the people who are performing a ministry that already exists. This will not always be possible, but people will be more receptive to change if you can retool existing ministries into new ministries.

Next, we suggest you consider the three things all ministries need to function: staff, stuff, and space. "Staff" refers to the people it will take to do the ministry. "Stuff" is the lesson books, chairs, vehicles, musical instruments, tools, or whatever materials are required for the ministry. "Space" is a place for the ministry to meet and to store its stuff between meetings. For each prospective ministry on your list, write down the staff, stuff, and space each will require.

Finally, you must decide what to actually begin. We will say more about this at the end of the chapter.

### Infrastructure Change

The infrastructure of a church, as we are using the term, is the framework through which decisions are made and ministry gets done. This could include a constitution, bylaws, policy manual, list of values, and mission and/or vision statement. A book could be written about each of these—and likely already has. It is not our purpose to go into great depth about each here, but rather to pass along a few tips that relate more specifically to town and country contexts.

First, let's remember that the kinds of documents we're talking about here are not "thus saith the Lord" documents. In other words, they are subject to change.

Second, let's consider why a change in infrastructure might be needed. There are many potential reasons:

- The present documents are old, and use archaic language. They need to be freshened up.

- Through the years much evolutionary change has taken place, and the documents need to catch up with current church practices.

- A change is needed due to inefficiency. A current process may be cumbersome or difficult to implement in a timely manner.

- A current decision-making process has proved to continually create conflict.

- The language of the present document is confusing.

- The church's understanding of a certain doctrine or biblical method has changed and needs to be reflected in its official documents.

- New ministries, situations, or personnel have arisen since the governance documents were written.

- The church's size has changed, and the present documents are no longer workable.

- The church is rather scattered or haphazard in its approach to ministry, or it lacks a sense of direction. A values, mission, and/or vision statement is needed. A number of good books have been written in recent years on such statements. If they are used with care (in particular, if they are contextualized to fit town and country ministry), they can make a big difference in your church.

Third, as stated earlier, one of the unique traits of town and country churches is the long tenure of its attenders. We need to be mindful as we rewrite the infrastructure document that we may be working with folks who wrote it originally, or who worked on a previous revision, or who voted for the previous document. We need to be careful about harshly criticizing the way things are worded. Instead, point out how new circumstances have arisen that make it advantageous to change the wording of the present document.

Fourth, be aware that every church has an actual infrastructure that invariably differs from the paper infrastructure. Changing the paper won't matter a bit if actual changes don't happen in practice. For *real* change to happen, we will need to work at changing both. Changing the actual infrastructure will take longer, and require patience and perseverance.

Fifth, be particularly sensitive to those who may face altered roles when the new infrastructure changes are implemented. This change could threaten their identity or perceived value. We need to monitor this closely.

Sixth, be sensitive to the fact that many rural cultures are more oral in nature. Written documents are less important in those contexts. Producing them can be perceived as a waste of time. The congregation might have the attitude, "Sure, pastor, go ahead and do this if you want to," but not really see the need for it. After it is completed, the newly created document might be ignored or put on a shelf somewhere and seldom if ever referred to, much less followed.

Seventh, consider cultural elements that might affect the process. Some of these were addressed in chapter two—such as some agrarians seeing the writing of a vision statement as presumptuous, or the need to take a more grassroots approach to decision making. We encourage you to review chapter two before beginning any infrastructure changes.

Some time ago, a pastor who had just a few months earlier begun his small-town ministry came to Ron quite disturbed and on the verge of resigning. He had read a number of books and taken a class on vision in his seminary. Before moving to his new town, he carefully formulated a vision for his soon-to-be church. Soon after beginning his ministry, he eagerly began to try to instill his vision in his leaders and congregation. His efforts were met with ambivalence and even some resistance. Frustrated, he asked Ron, "How can I pastor this church if they are not willing to follow my vision?" Ron suspected that behind this was a question even more troubling: "How can I pastor this church if they are not willing to follow my leadership?" This pastor found himself in a quandary because he had not adequately contextualized his change process. Ron encouraged this pastor to get to know his people and culture better before trying to infuse vision.

There may not always be need for infrastructure changes, but we would do well to continually evaluate whether changes are needed. When we sense the infrastructure is getting in the way of accomplishing the work

Christ left His church on earth to do, it must be changed. Changing the paper document may take months, and changing thought patterns may take years, but infrastructure can be changed in the town and country church, and the ministry benefits that result will be worth the effort.

## Facility Change

Of all the changes, perhaps the one that tends to generate the greatest emotion and controversy in town and country areas is a change to the church building, anything from paint or carpet to the construction of a new building. Most Christians agree with the fact that church buildings are temporary, that buildings are a tool for ministry, that the building is not the church, that clinging to right doctrine ranks higher in importance than clinging to a building . . . yet some lose perspective when church building changes are proposed.

Those who lead town and country churches through change must understand that many in their congregations will have strong emotional ties to their church building. Reasons for this include: (1) Church buildings represent history, memories, and shared experiences that go far beyond the bricks and boards. Many rural people can look back on several generations of family and community history that unfolded in their church building. This is a contrast to churches in suburbs, where residents are more transient. (2) Church buildings represent considerable sacrifice. Whereas in suburban churches "sacrifice" tends to solely mean "money," in rural churches sacrifice also means time. Because rural people are do-it-yourselfers, a part of their lives was invested in the building. (3) Church buildings represent community. Historically, town and country churches have been the primary gathering place, the relational hub in the community. This translates into a lot of value being placed in the church buildings where relationships were fostered. For these reasons and more, proposing building changes is serious business for those who are leading their church through change.

Collectively, the three of us have considerable experience with the agonies and ecstasies of building changes. We have been involved in a complete relocation, five building additions, six fairly major remodeling projects, and the construction of a church-owned nursing home—all in town and country locations. After devoting thousands of man-hours to both the planning and the construction itself (yes, we've swung more than a hammer or two!), fielding dozens of objections and arbitrating dozens of conflicts, and raising and spending millions of dollars, we offer the following collective wisdom concerning changes to church buildings.

- A well-maintained facility sends a message to the community that the church is important to those who attend. Neglected mainte-nance is not only financially costly because it will lead to major repairs down the road, it is spiritually costly because it sends a message to the community that the church is not a high priority.

- Long-time attenders may focus so much on relationships that they fail to notice the peeling paint, crumbling sidewalks, yellowed curtains, and worn fixtures. In their eyes, the church building is attractive because it is the place that elicits strong feelings about people. But newcomers do not share this perspective. A neg-lected church building sends the message to newcomers, accu-rate or not, that whatever significant experiences may have hap-pened there in the past, nothing of significance is happening there now.

- It might be tempting to give more attention to worship and Christian education space while neglecting such things as the nursery, rest rooms, and handicap accessibility. The latter are also important, especially in the eyes of newcomers.

- In most cases, smaller changes need to precede major changes. Small steps like applying some fresh paint to what exists, or replacing broken windows or worn trim, or refinishing aging fur-nishings will help prime the pump for bigger changes and, in the process, will generate credibility for the leaders.

- The notion, "If we build it they will come," seldom is a wise course of direction for the town and country church. In a place where practicality reigns, it is best that a clear need drive any decision to tackle a building project.

- Due to the practical and frugal nature of rural people, it is gener-ally important that all reasonable solutions to space problems be explored. Before moving in the direction of erecting a new build-ing, consider going to two services, tearing out a few walls, recon-figuring the seating, or renting a building next door.

- Pressed by economic uncertainties, many rural people will not vote for a building project if debt is involved. This means that lead-ers will need to be patient. With a pay-as-you-go plan, a building project in town and country areas will likely proceed at a much slower pace than in the cities. If it is apparent that debt is unavoid-able, inevitably someone will say, "We don't want to leave debt to our children." A seasoned rural pastor shared with us this good answer: "We could wait for our church building to fall down and then leave all the debt for our children, or we could help them with the debt now."

- Before congregational ownership of a building project is achieved, the endorsement of key individuals will be of critical importance. These will likely include (1) matriarchs and patriarchs who sacrificed greatly for the present facility but see the need for a change, (2) key influencers, highly respected individuals that the congregation commonly looks to for approval on major decisions, (3) the church treasurer, who not only keeps the books but serves as the guardian of the church's money ("If Harvey says we have the money to do it, then let's do it."), and (4) the church "brakeman" who stands ready at the brakes to prevent the train from moving dangerously fast or taking the wrong track.

- Remember that rural people may want to give more than money to a building project. Some will want to give time, talents, and use of any machinery they own, and that could translate into a bigger gift than money.

- If part of a building is being dismantled, special care should be taken to preserve remnants that have historical significance. Perhaps some of the woodwork or furnishings in the old building can be preserved and given a place of honor in the new.

- Careful preemptive attention needs to be given to the prospect of items donated or purchased as memorials. Decisions regarding such items should be made by a committee so that no one person is saddled with any discontent that might arise. The committee needs to develop a printed set of criteria for accepting, or not accepting, donated items. The committee needs to determine whether and how these donated items will be recognized. (Does the church want little brass plates all over the building?) It needs to plan a communication strategy so that the congregation will understand that donated items must serve the ministry purposes of the congregation and that when donated items have out-lived their usefulness they will be replaced.

## Small Changes Add Up

As we observe town and country churches, including the ones we have served, seldom do we see one big change that needs to be made. Most often it's a lot of little things that need to happen, which, added up over time, make a huge difference: A gallon of paint in the church kitchen. Some tweaking of the children's program. A new look for the church bulletin. A slightly different approach to worship.

Here is a manageable approach to addressing such change. First, make a list of all the changes that come to mind that you think would be beneficial. Don't be surprised if, when you are done, your list is long and daunting.

Next, place each of these needed changes under one of the four categories discussed above. If it's developing your preaching skills, put it under "personal change." If it's adding a youth ministry, put it under "ministry change." If it's writing a mission statement, put it under "infrastructure change." If it's painting the church kitchen, put it under "facility change."

At this point you may be overwhelmed with all the changes that you see need to happen. Don't let the big picture discourage you. Remember that change in the town and country church is a marathon, not a sprint. Instead of being overwhelmed, view your list as bite-sized chunks.

Start by prioritizing the changes needed in each of the four categories. When you prioritize, don't necessarily make the most important change the first change on your list. (You may want to read that last sentence again.) Before tackling some of the more important or challenging changes, build momentum and trust by starting with some of the obvious changes that most everyone can see need to happen, or some of the simpler and more doable changes that won't be hard to accomplish, or some of the less controversial changes.

Now, see if some of the changes on your list need to be done in stages, for instance, worship changes. In order to get from where you are to where you think the church should ultimately be, you may want to take several steps. Insert these steps into your list.

Next, put your changes on a schedule—a realistic schedule. Then begin to whittle away at them one by one. Tackle one change in each of the four categories at a time, starting with the change that is at the top of your list in each category and working down from there.

If you take this approach to change, we believe that you will soon be amazed at the progress and difference you see in your church!

## Changes Overlap

The four areas of change in this chapter are not as compartmentalized as one might think. What recently happened in a small-town church illustrates this. Because of unique circumstances in his life, a seasoned ministry colleague had a few months of down time. A pastor-friend of his who was in a challenging small-town ministry perceptively saw the value that this man could be to his church and invited him to serve alongside him for a few months.

One of the things this short-term church leader decided to do was set a goal of making at least one visible mini-change to the facility every week. He painted a banister white (it had been an unattractive brown color). He removed the ugly carpet from the steps leading to the office. With the help of others, some unused equipment from the platform area was moved. A banner was hung in the back of the sanctuary. A small and affordable sound system was added. The literature table was cleaned up. A stained spot on the ceiling was painted. Some ceiling tile that was coming down was nailed up. A coat of paint was put on the nursery shelving. Nursery toys that were well worn were thrown out.

These facility changes resulted in more than just an improved appearance. People in the church began to be moved from their status quo position. There was a growing sense that "change is possible" and that, in fact, "change is happening." This helped produce energy for ministry and infrastructure changes, such as changes in the worship format and the formulation of a vision for the church.

After several months this servant-leader moved on, but the pastor and other leaders in the church continued to effect changes, some quite significant. Walls in the basement have been torn out and new ones built in more appropriate places. The fellowship hall has been expanded. Work has been done to bring the building up to code. Beyond building changes, other changes continue to happen as well, such as the recent launching of a children's program.

Mini-changes help pave the way for more changes, and sometimes bigger changes. One change leads to another . . . and another, until a whole series of changes have occurred. When, over time, church leaders have faithfully devoted themselves to incremental, evolutionary changes, they will be able to look back and see that nothing short of *big* change has come to their small-town church.

We've seen the need. We've committed ourselves to a careful process. We've identified a plethora of changes that need to be made. We've prioritized these changes. All that remains is leading our church through change. How do we do so? First, we'll address the spiritual steps.

CHAPTER EIGHT

# Spiritual Steps Leading to Change

**THE LAST THING THE CHURCH NEEDS**—especially the town and country church—is another book on church leadership that combines pop sociology and corporate management concepts and pronounces itself a book about church leadership. We believe that leading any church is essentially a theological task, guided by the Word and empowered by the Spirit. In chapter nine we will suggest some contextual steps that might be used to facilitate change, gleaned from our observation, experience, and the social sciences. But first, there are several spiritual steps that we should consider.

Jesus did not call the leaders of His church generals, coaches, or CEOs. He called them shepherds. A shepherd's task and calling is to gently and carefully lead sheep. Sometimes this means leading them to new pastures and fresh streams as old ones wither and dry up. Sometimes it means leading away from danger. But leading always implies movement, and movement means change. A shepherd's task, then, is to lead the sheep safely through change, whether planned or unexpected.

Change in the church is as old as the church itself. When the church held its first preaching service on the day of Pentecost, it numbered about 120. At the end of the day it numbered about 3,120. A 26-fold increase certainly counts as a change! This forced another change: Prior to that time the disciples had met as one group; now they would have to meet from house to house—a change from one "service" to multiple services.

As the church continued to grow, other changes confronted the leaders. When the numbers grew to the point that some of the members were not being ministered to the way they should have been, the apostles had to change the way ministry was done, prioritizing the ministry of the Word and prayer for themselves and delegating the care for physical needs to seven men selected for this service. You could say they changed from generalized to specialized ministry and that they created new "staff" positions.

When the church grew to the point where it included Gentiles, it faced yet another change: it had to sort out ethnic and cultural distinctives from true spiritual matters. Because culture and history were so intertwined with theology, it took considerable thought, discussion, and searching of the Scriptures for the church to determine which of its current practices were essentials that could never be abandoned and which did not need to be required of newcomers. Not everyone agreed with the outcome of the meeting in Jerusalem, and that fact in itself produced some changes in the church.

Change has been a part of the church from its earliest days. The church's first leaders (shepherds) navigated these changes not by clever appropriations of worldly wisdom but by solid spiritual principles. We would do well to follow their examples.

## Step One: Prayer

It was the third Thursday of the month, and, as the sun went down, it was time for the monthly board meeting at Logger's Grove Church. Wilbur, the board chair, called the meeting to order, and the members stood without being told to do so. Wilbur said, "Let us pray. Dear Lord we thank you for the beautiful day and the rain we had yesterday please watch over the growing crop and bless our meeting Amen." As they sat down Wilbur said, "The first thing we need to talk about tonight . . ."

All over, church leaders coming together to make decisions begin their meetings like this—a nod and wave to Jesus as they get down to the "real" business. But Jesus *is* the real business, and the most important step in leading the church through change is to seek His heart about what change is needed and how it is best accomplished. Beginning any other way will likely take us in the wrong direction.

Consider the position of the church in Acts 4. Peter and John had just been threatened by the Sanhedrin and told not to preach. The church was facing change by coercion (government regulation) and quite likely displacement (the jailing or killing of these leaders). The response was not to call an attorney or even a board meeting. They called a prayer meeting. They prayed not that God would protect them but that they would be bold in doing what He wanted. "And the place where they were meeting was shaken!"

Further, it wasn't just Peter and John who prayed, but the church. When we not only pray as leaders for direction but also lead our church in prayer for direction, then the entire church is, together, starting on the right path toward change and collectively preparing itself to walk that path.

Years ago Ron pastored a small-town church that had a storied history of sending out missionaries. But this had slowed in recent years, which prompted considerable discussion among the missions committee members. This discussion led to prayer—as individuals, at their meetings, and during corporate services.

After much prayer the committee decided they wanted to encourage youth to go on summer missions trips. In those days youth going on such trips was a relatively new idea, in other words, a change. What would parents think about sending their kids a long way from home? Would church people think their leaders had a few loose screws, advocating the church financially support pleasure trips for its kids? The committee was apprehensive, but it moved forward. Members started talking with youth leaders and young people. Much to their pleasant surprise, about a dozen wanted to go.

The missions committee, along with the church board, had committed themselves to raising a significant percentage of the funds. When a dozen youth signed up, the reality of this commitment set in. Ron recalls a meeting when the missions committee, Ron included, sat around the table with paralyzing fear. So much money was needed that they questioned whether the actual amount should be communicated to the congregation for fear that it would overwhelm them.

After a long silence someone on the committee suggested, "We ought to pray about this." After praying, with feeble voice Ron said to the committee, "You know, God seems to be in this. We challenged the young people to go on a summer missions trip. We were hoping 1 or 2 would respond, 12 have responded. God seems to be working in the hearts of the young people. Maybe He will work in the hearts of others to give."

The committee gave Ron the green light to go to the congregation. He hoped the choir standing behind him wasn't noticing his shaking knees as he shared the need before the entire church. Then, in that service, the church prayed.

What followed was one of the greatest workings of God that Ron has experienced in ministry. The congregation responded generously to God's promptings. The money was raised in three weeks' time without any heavy-handed tactics. The youth had a spectacular summer. They came back with such enthusiastic reports that the next year another group of teens went. In addition, adults young and old started to go. In about three years' time, more than 30 went on trips. During that time, three couples chose missions as their permanent vocation.

And it all started with prayer.

## Step Two: Preparatory Preaching and Teaching

The preacher has a unique instrument to effect change. Although preachers almost always lack political or economic power, they have in the Word of God the power to convict, persuade, and convince. While politics and economics will fail to hold people's hearts beyond the next promise or payday, God's Word pierces to the heart, dividing soul and spirit, and thereby prompts changes in people's thinking and attitudes. God has promised that His Word is powerful and will not fail to do its work. When God is leading His people to make a change, His Word will provide instructions regarding that change.

Preparatory preaching and teaching comes in two phases. The first is a general, consistent exposition of the Bible. A congregation well fed on the meat of the Word will be more spiritually prepared to discern where God is leading. The second phase kicks in when the shepherd sees a change coming: Prepare the congregation by preaching and teaching on themes and texts that will lay a solid foundation for the change.

Our Lord did this. His Great Commission in Matthew 28:19-20 and subsequent teaching in Acts 1:8 prepared the church for what happened later in Acts 10 and 15, and much of the remainder of Acts, as the church reached out to non-Jews. This was preparatory preaching and teaching.

Some examples for today: If a change in the worship format is in the works, preach well ahead of time on such things as the meaning of worship, the diversity of worship expressions in Scripture, and some cautions about "offering strange fire" (Leviticus 10:1-2). If there is a growing burden to reach a new ethnic group that has settled in town, sermons on the Good Samaritan or from 1 Corinthians 9 would be good starting places. Doing this kind of preaching will give the congregation a biblical framework for being discerning regarding an anticipated change.

Preparatory preaching and teaching is not something you start to do three weeks before a change is implemented. The more drastic the change, the further ahead it should begin to be addressed—not every week, but from time to time. As people see how the Word challenges their assumptions or the status quo, the Holy Spirit will begin to create dissatisfaction and even a discomfort within the hearts of the congregation.

This is not to suggest that the Bible should be used as a club to persuade people to make a change. Nor does this mean that every change a church might need to make has a proof text. One dear saint cited Paul's escape from Damascus in a basket as proof that God wanted her church to help smuggle Bibles into closed countries. God might want this, but that text does not make the case. The Bible will not tell us what color our carpet should be or if we should sing from books or a screen, but it will tell us how we should treat each other as the decision is being made. The Word is the most powerful tool you have to effect change, but use it "as a workman who does not need to be ashamed and who correctly handles the word of truth" (2 Timothy 2:15 NIV).

## Step Three: Build Loving Relationships

It should go without saying that healthy Christianity is about loving relationships and shepherds should love their flocks. Do we even need to provide texts to substantiate this? Yet, too often in teaching the theories and skills of ministry we overlook this basic task of the shepherd. Loving relationships within a congregation, modeled by the leaders, are essential for leading change. While we believe that these relationships are important everywhere, the relational orientation of small-town people makes this utterly indispensable.

Small-town people may be concerned about their leaders' level of education, skills, decision-making capabilities, and persuasive powers; however, healthy relationships between leaders and congregation trump all of these. If relationships are intact, then the congregation will be much more responsive to their leaders' proposals for change. If those in leadership positions try to bring change apart from healthy relationships, they are setting themselves up for failure.

A key to leading through change, then, is leading through relationships. If the quality of relationships isn't there, put the proposed change on hold and concentrate on strengthening the relationships. Unfortunately, many town and country pastors and leaders do not understand the importance of this. They are taught in school or in a seminar how to be change agents, or they take their cues from larger, suburban churches whose members are less likely to know their pastors and leaders well. They try to bring change using persuasive arguments, or impressive presentations, or a more autocratic approach. They try to do an end-run around relationship building. And they fail to lead change.

Relationships in the small-town church are the forerunner to change. If through building relationships the congregation has grown to love you, and trust and respect you, then they are much more likely to follow your leadership through change. In the absence of loving relationships, it does not matter how good your ideas are—they simply will not fly.

While we're talking about relationships, it's helpful to understand that rural people live in an intricate web of human relationships. Think of each relationship as a cord tying two people together. While residents of metropolitan areas may have one or two cords tying them to someone else in their community or church, rural residents have dozens, even hundreds.

Let's imagine two churches, one in a large suburb and the other in a small town. In the suburban church two leaders find themselves conflicted over a change in the church's worship format. These two men work for different companies, in different parts of the city; their children attend different schools; and their wives shop in different stores. Except for a few hours in church each week, their paths never cross. The conflict between them affects only their relationship within the church.

Contrast this with the same situation in a rural church. Once again, the two leaders are conflicted over worship style. But in the rural church these two fellows may be related by blood or marriage (sometimes both!), their children attend the same schools and participate in the same extracurricular activities, and their wives shop in the same stores. These men are likely to serve together on a community board or two, belong to the same clubs, have each other as business customers, and depend on each other for emergency services such as firefighting and medical assistance. On and on it goes. This is why, if a conflict is going on in your church, someone who does not attend your church may approach you on the street and say, "I wish you would get that fight worked out; you're messing up my bowling team."

People in rural communities are typically connected to each other in dozens of ways. These connections form intricate webs of relationships that are constantly in a dynamic tension. When conflict is introduced into any one relationship, it reverberates throughout the entire web, shaking everybody up. This is one reason why many rural people are hesitant to initiate change:  it introduces conflict into their web of relationships. It is our theory that conflicts are often resolved by the expulsion of the person with the fewest connections in the web (often the pastor), even if others bear more responsibility for the conflict.

Because of this, it is crucial that the new pastor and other newcomers who may be future leaders of change in a rural church invest considerable time, years perhaps, building themselves into the web. This is done by providing pastoral care in times of crisis, visiting the elderly in their homes, practicing hospitality, spending time in the local café, attending community events, and generally being a friend to people in the church and community. Once you are solidly a part of the web, the church will have to resolve its conflicts where they actually exist and not by deflecting them onto you. Only then is it likely you will be able to lead through change in the church.

We must be careful, however. Building one's self into the web is not to be merely a technique to manipulate change. Rural folks will see right through this phony motive. The point is that the right way to be a leader, change or no change, is to genuinely want to take time to get to know people.

## Step Four: One-to-One Communication with Decision Makers

This step may not seem, at first glance, like it belongs in the chapter titled "Spiritual Steps." But we include it here because, at its heart, this step is about the biblical character traits of patience and humility. This step requires that you go slowly, taking the time to privately discuss your view of needed changes with each decision maker in the church. Obviously this takes patience. Why it takes humility will be seen after we first consider some reasons for taking this step.

In Acts 10:9-16 the Lord had a personal conversation with Peter about what was soon to be one of the most massive changes the church would ever see: the inclusion of the Gentiles. He took time to engage with Peter about the change before going public with the change.

A physical reason to talk individually with rural people, especially men, is that a disproportionate number of them suffer hearing loss as a result of years of outdoor work around loud machinery. This is particularly true of those over 40, who will often comprise a majority of the decision making group.

A psychological reason for discussing a new idea privately with key individuals before presenting it publicly is to make sure the idea is understood. If you publicly present an idea that involves terms or concepts that some may not understand, they may simply oppose the idea rather than ask questions. Another segment of rural people may be uncomfortable asking questions in a group. They will, however, willingly ask questions one-on-one.

An attitudinal reason for talking with individuals is to show respect for their opinions and input. You may well find, as you listen to their response, that they have some valid objections or improvements to suggest. In this way they become full participants in the pre-meeting consensus process.

A cultural reason for talking to individuals ahead of time is that it's the rural way. Rural people are accustomed to a grassroots approach: bottom-up rather than top-down. Ultimately decisions are not made in formal meetings. If decisions are supposedly made in a meeting, with no grassroots work done ahead of time, the decision may well be meaningless.

Ron, being of city background, came to understand this the hard way. He was accustomed to a more top-down approach. This made him frustrated with his congregation when in meetings a decision would pass easily, without dissension, but later Ron would find that people didn't like the decision, or they ignored it, or even reversed it.

Then Ron began to observe what happened in the "meetings after the meeting." After the formal meeting ended, the informal meetings began. Some took place in the foyer on the way out of church. Some the next day in the café. Some on the phone.

Grappling with the new-found realization that decisions in rural communities are made on the grassroots level through informal means, Ron thought, *There has to be a way to let this process happen before a vote, so we don't have to go through the pain of formally approving a decision only to have it informally rejected.* From this he began to realize the importance of talking with people one-on-one ahead of time.

Because the one-on-one method is the rural way, if a new idea is first presented in a group meeting and not individually, everybody may think they are the only one who was left out of the loop. You may even hear them ask others immediately following the meeting, "Had you heard about this?" They may take offense, thinking they had been overlooked.

This process of one-on-one communication requires the biblical character quality of humility. It takes humility to be willing to listen to others and be teachable. It takes humility when you realize that not everyone is quick to see your "great idea" as a great idea. It takes humility to see the seeds you planted in personal discussions surface as the great idea of someone to whom you introduced the concept. Most of all, it takes humility to enter into the process and at some point in your discussions with others realize that your idea wasn't really very good, or that it could be improved upon considerably, and admit that you were headed toward making a big mistake. These decision makers have an understanding of the culture and community that you may never have, and, to paraphrase the Apostle Paul, they too have the Holy Spirit.

We have suggested that leading the church toward change should begin by following the biblical metaphor of being a good shepherd. A good shepherd proceeds cautiously and carefully, after much prayer. A good shepherd does not drive the sheep (a top-down approach) but gently leads them, and leads them as one who knows each sheep individually (John 10:14).

The four steps outlined above are some of the spiritual steps to consider as we lead our church toward change. These steps set us on a solid foundation for the steps outlined in the next chapter, which are more cultural in nature.

## CHAPTER NINE

# Cultural Steps Leading to Change

**RURAL CULTURE IS DISTINCTIVE**. As chapter two discussed, agrarians significantly differ from cosmopolitans in a number of ways. Whereas the previous chapter's steps grew out of the essential nature of our work as shepherds of Christ's church, the following steps grow out of the distinctive aspects of the rural culture.

### Step Five: Rely on Key Persuaders and Diplomats

Barney's church had long needed additional education space. For three years the leaders had studied, analyzed, and finally reached a consensus that a classroom addition was something that should be done. All of the official channels of the church had given their nod of approval, but it still had to pass a congregational vote. Because it would be expensive, it was unclear how the vote would turn out.

At the congregational meeting various people spoke, some in support, some with caution. Then Mary Katherine stood up—an older lady, retired, who devoted most of her time to caring for her aged mother and aunt. She had been the nurse at the doctor's office in town and, at one time or another, had cared for most of the people who were present at the meeting. Her recent life had not been easy. She hadn't attended a church business meeting in years, but she came that night. She sat near the back with a bag of yarn and crocheted quietly as the issue was batted back and forth.

When it finally seemed that no one else had anything to say, Mary Katherine laid aside her hooks and yarn, stood up, and spoke: "I don't get to church as much as I used to, and I don't teach Sunday school any more, but I used to, and I've taught a lot of you, and we need these class-rooms." She sat back down and quietly went back to crocheting. The proposition to build passed unanimously.

Mary Katherine was what we call a "key persuader." She held no office in the church and had not been a participant in previous discussions, but she had the moral authority to be heard and respected, and the longevity to be trusted. In a rural culture, those two things are especially important. Key persuaders are a great asset to the change process. Their support lends credibility and a blessing to the change.

Finding key persuaders is not easy, and they may not be the first people that come to mind. You can sometimes spot a key persuader by being observant. When a new idea is voiced in a meeting, watch to see who everyone turns to look at, and try to discern why. If they regularly turn to the same person and the results are consistently wise counsel, that may be a key persuader.

Notice however that in the story above Mary Katherine was never a part of the regular deliberations. She came out of the relative obscurity of the back pew, with no one's advance knowledge, at just the right time. She was an answer to prayer. The best way to find a key persuader for your change issue is to ask God for this person and let Him take care of it.

More visible than the key persuaders are the diplomats. These folks also have the long history and moral authority to hold respect, but their function is different. They move easily among the church's various con-stituencies, explaining, answering questions, clearing up misconceptions, and smoothing ruffled feathers. Diplomats are almost always part of the official decision-making group of the church. They tend to be gregarious, friendly folks who smile and tell stories. Unlike key persuaders, diplomats can be recruited and even asked to speak with individuals or groups about the change.

## Step Six: Identify Similar Innovators

Decades ago, the United States Department of Agriculture wanted to introduce a change to farming: a move from open-pollinated corn to hybrid seed corn. To convince farmers to make this change, they commis-sioned an army of County Extension agents. The agents developed a simple but effective strategy. They knew the change would benefit the farmers, but they also knew that words alone would not persuade many to try the new corn. They could, however, persuade a few. After these few had successful harvests, the county agents would take other farmers around on a tour to the innovative farms. The agents would introduce the farmers to each other, then step back and let them talk together. When the farmers heard of the benefits of this innovation from someone just like themselves, many more began to use the hybrid seed. The agents could have talked until they were blue in the face and never convinced the farmers, but a testimonial from one of their own made the change desirable.

The same strategy will work for agrarian churches. If you want to start a second worship service or add on a multi-purpose room, gather some leaders from your church and take them to see the innovation in another *rural* church. Telling them a church in a big city is doing this won't carry any weight. They need to see folks they identify as "just like us" who have made this idea work. Be sure there's time for visiting and questions. This simple step will have an amazing effect upon gaining acceptance of the change.

### Step Seven: Use History and Tradition

Roy Underhill, author of the Woodwright's Shop series of how-to books and star of the PBS series by the same name, tells a story every church leader should hear. An old farmer had two impatient sons. Each year when the new hay crop came in, the sons would have to carry the bales from the door of the hay mow to the back of the loft. In the middle of the loft was a huge beam running across the width of the barn. It was too high to step over and too low to duck under, and, with every trip the boys made with the heavy bales, the beam irritated them more and more.

One summer day, while waiting for another wagon-load of hay to arrive, the boys decided to end their frustration and remove the offensive beam. They found a two-man saw and gleefully began sawing. As the saw teeth cut through the last bit of the beam, the boys were delighted to at last be free of the beam that had for so long held them back. Then, with a crack, a groan, and a mighty crash, the barn collapsed! The moral of this story is "Don't try to remove a tradition when it is serving a useful purpose."[5]

Many church leaders look at the history and traditions of a rural church like those boys looked at the beam: an offensive obstacle thwarting work and progress. They undertake the dangerous task of removing traditions when perhaps the best course is to rely on them. Learning the history and traditions of the congregation may give you a harness to hitch

---

[2]Roy Underhill, *The Woodwright's Eclectic Workshop* (Chapel Hill: University of North Carolina Press, 1991), pg 54.

the past to the future. Such a connection lends a precedent for the change and confirms that it stands solidly in the best tradition of the congregation. Two examples illustrate this.

Started in a one-room schoolhouse by prairie farmers, the church Barney pastors, the Walnut Grove Church, built its first simple frame building in 1889. In the 1920s the church remodeled and merged with another congregation. In the late 1940s they tore down the building and used the old lumber along with some new to build a larger building. In the late 1960s they added some Sunday school classrooms. When in the early 1990s they considered adding more space (mentioned above in the story of Mary Katherine), one thing people said was, "It's time to build again!" The fact that the church had expanded every couple of decades made the current building plans not so much a change as a continuing part of its history and tradition.

When displaced persons from Southeast Asia began arriving in the United States after the Vietnam War, the government asked churches in rural America to take them in. In many congregations the younger folks were hesitant to get involved because doing so seemed new and strange to them, a real change from anything they had ever known. It was their grandparents, who remembered getting off the boat at Ellis Island with nothing but what little they could carry, that reminded the rural churches in the upper Midwest and Great Plains that they were once immigrants themselves and someone made a place for them. Congregations of blonde, blue-eyed Scandinavians welcomed the dark-haird, brown-eyed Asians, not because they looked alike, talked alike, or thought alike, but because they were fellow immigrants and "this has always been an immigrant church."

Learn what your congregation is proud of from its past. Learn about the times when they think they were at their best. Help them see the change they need to make as being another step along that path.

## Step Eight: Sample the Change

Harry Miller stood in the partially harvested cornfield and gazed forlornly at his combine. Now in its eighth season, the big machine had just broken down, and this time it was serious. It couldn't be fixed in the field and he couldn't move it, so he had to call the dealer in town to come with a flatbed to haul it in. To make matters worse, rains were forecast for later in the week. Forty-five minutes later a big semi rumbled to a stop alongside the field to pick up the immobile combine. To Harry's surprise, the truck carried a new combine. The dealer climbed from the truck and shook hands with Harry. "Know there's rain coming," he said. "I thought you could use this one until we get yours fixed."

As his old machine was hauled away to the shop, Harry started up the new one. He was surprised at how much faster this model made its way through the corn and how much more comfortable it was. Harry finished his harvest with the new combine and a week later signed the papers to buy it.

The implement dealer understood step eight: try the change with a no-risk, money-back guarantee. In other words, sample the change. If you want to add a second service, try it for a month or two with the promise that if it doesn't work the service will be discontinued. If you think you need to add a staff member, try hiring a seminary student for the summer. Admittedly there is some danger in making a change reversible. After doing so, some may want to do just that—reverse it. But if it's a good change, the majority will likely embrace the change. If the majority prefers the new way, the change will probably happen more smoothly and be a lasting one.

Not every change can or should be reversed. If a building has to be torn down or walls ripped out to allow for an expansion, this obviously cannot be reversed. Sometimes the leadership may think a change in policy or program is so essential that reverting back should not be an option. But when you can let the congregation sample the change without a full-blown commitment, it may make the change smoother.

**Step Nine: Evaluate**

The final step is to evaluate the effectiveness of the change. In evaluating, look for three things: (1) Did the change accomplish what we had hoped? (2) Did it have effects we did not intend? (3) Can we sustain the change?

First, we make changes to accomplish some agreed-upon purpose. Before a change is initiated, establish clear, specific goals and write them down. After the change has taken effect and some time has passed for it to settle in, evaluate whether each goal was reached. Some goals will be easier to measure than others. The length of time needed before evaluation will vary with the nature of the change.

Second, every change is subject to the Law of Unintended Consequences. Change theorists, those who study change and its effects, have long observed that changes produce effects that were not intended or foreseen by those who initiated them. These consequences may be beneficial or adverse, or both. Building additions will change traffic patterns and the desirability of certain rooms for meetings—some good, some perhaps not so good. Changes in worship service format or time may simultaneously attract unexpected people and cause others to stay away. Changes in governance structures almost always create unforeseen power vacuums and areas of ministry left unassigned. After the change is made, explore its unintended consequences, looking for how the negative ones can be minimized and the positive ones maximized.

Finally, sometimes a change can produce beneficial results that please almost everyone, but take too much money, time, or people to sustain. Determine whether it is possible to adjust the change to make it sustainable while still producing the intended effects. In some cases desired changes need to be reversed until the necessary assets become available.

## It Takes Time

In this chapter and the previous one we have laid out nine steps for leading a church through an intentional change. We offer these steps as the distilled essence of our experience and study. Step one (prayer) should always come first. The next three (preparatory preaching and teaching, building relationships, and one-to-one communication) should also be near the beginning. The cultural steps described in this chapter can occur in any order and often simultaneously. Evaluation must be last, as it can only come after the change has been made. Every change may not require every step.

It takes time to go through these steps. Building the kind of relationships needed to lead through change in this manner requires a long-term commitment. Short tenures, particularly short pastoral tenures, will hinder leaders from developing the kind of relationships needed for facilitating change. Many rural churches serve as training grounds for seminary students or newly ordained pastors who stay two or three years and then move on. Often these churches have learned some negative lessons from this rapid succession in shepherds. One is that their congregation is inferior to others. Feeling repeatedly abandoned for a "better" church creates a negative self-image and makes the church less willing to trust the next pastor and less confidant about its ability to change. Like a person who has been repeatedly jilted, church members can become bitter and withdraw emotionally. As the time draws near when pastors usually move on congregations may even turn against their shepherd as a defense mechanism for another anticipated rejection.

A lesson churches learn from repeated short-term pastorates is to wait out the changes the current pastor wants to lead. Why go through making a five-year plan when no pastor ever stays to implement it? The folks in these churches will smile and nod and rarely, if ever, object to the changes a new pastor wants to plan, but neither will they commit to them. This may sound mildly passive-aggressive; it probably is.

To overcome a congregation's previous disappointments and related distrust, a shepherd should settle in for the long haul. While a shepherd might be successful at implementing some changes early on, in many churches it will take at least five years for a congregation to begin really trusting their pastor to the point that they are willing to be led through significant change. In churches that have been wounded by a string of "love 'em and leave 'em" shepherds, it could take even longer.

## It Is Time

There is no time like the present to lead your church through change. Many of you have already been doing so, and doing it well. We hope this book has provided insights and practical pointers that will encourage you to stay the course and keep you on track with bringing change to your church. Others of you who are reading this perhaps have sensed the need for change but are not very far along in the process. We hope this book will help provide the impetus you need to get started on this exciting and adventure-filled journey, as well as a roadmap that will guide you every step of the way.

Please don't stop reading just yet. You might find that the pages to follow are the most interesting in the entire book.

EPILOGUE

# Expect Deliverance

**SOMETIMES WHEN WE ATTEMPT TO LEAD** through change, the resistance seems impossible to overcome. All the books on change ever written, including this one, are inadequate to get the job done. In such situations, more than anything else, we need to pray. Ask God for deliverance and then watch for it to happen. When we begin to move toward change and difficulties come (which is inevitable), lean on God to deliver and wait on Him to do it. We preach that God is a deliverer (e.g., Psalm 18), but do we trust Him to do it?

In order for change to happen, we need God to change minds. Or to move someone out of, or into, our church. Or to provide funds. Sometimes it takes awhile, and we have to be patient. In our instant-gratification society we want 24-hour (or maybe 24-minute) deliverance, but it almost always takes longer than that. Ultimately, if God wants the change to happen, He will provide.

A number of years ago a pastor-friend, "Larry," began serving a country church that had been in existence for more than 100 years. It was a good church, with a rich history, and Larry felt privileged to be chosen as its next pastor. Lo and behold, God used Larry to successfully lead the church through considerable change and in the process blessed it with sizable numerical growth. Despite multiple services, there was no more room in the sanctuary. Building a new sanctuary seemed out of the question because the old sanctuary was a classic historical building and a high percentage of the people in the church wanted to continue worshiping there. Some had seen several generations of baptisms, marriages, and funerals in that building.

Larry and the other church leaders found themselves in a quandary. They sympathized with the sizable number of congregants, dear and godly people, who had a deep attachment to that old sanctuary. It was not the leaders' desire to cause hard feelings or disrupt the unity of the church. Yet at the same time it was not their desire to stymie the growth God had been bringing. They found themselves in a situation where change was needed, but it was being resisted. There appeared to be no solution.

Rather than try to force change, Larry waited. While waiting, he continued to serve faithfully.

Larry continued to wait.

And wait.

Until one night a huge thunderstorm swept through the area, and lightning struck the sanctuary and burned it to the ground. Amazingly, firefighters were able to contain the fire to the old sanctuary building. A newer addition attached to the old sanctuary was saved, and for over a year the church held services in the fellowship hall of that newer addition until they were able to build a new sanctuary.

Change happened!

The cost of building a new sanctuary would have been overwhelming. However, this church had replacement value insurance. Their insurance company delivered a check for well over one million dollars, which covered much of the cost of the new sanctuary! This country church continues to grow to this day. In fact, they are now in the beginning stages of building another new sanctuary.

God may not use lightning, but sometimes there is only one way that change will happen, and that is through the deliverance of God. Stay faithful until that day comes, and live and serve expectantly.

Expect deliverance.

# TRUE STORIES OF CHANGE

**WE THOUGHT IT WOULD BE ENCOURAGING** and help-ful to conclude with some anecdotes about leading through change. These true stories come from our own personal experiences. They high-light and flesh out some of the principles and steps that we have shared in this book.

Four very different scenarios follow.

# Change in Worship Style

Marty has had two experiences of leading small-town churches through a change in worship style. The first occurred at First Baptist Church of Parkers Prairie, Minnesota (population: 900), which had not experienced a substantial change in worship style during its 120 years of existence. Although still functional, the standard order of hymns, announcements, offering, and sermon no longer adequately fulfilled the worship desires of a growing, younger congregation. With Marty's assistance and research, and after much prayer and discussion, the leaders of the church reached a consensus on how to approach the situation.

Over a three-month period, Marty preached a series of sermons on worship that laid the theological groundwork for the envisioned change in worship style. A worship team consisting of vocalists, guitar players and a pianist was recruited and began weekly rehearsals. The team contacted other churches for suggestions and worked together to select worship songs. Particular attention was given to their biblical message and how each song might be wisely introduced to the congregation.

Prior to the worship team's first Sunday up front, Marty explained the role of the worship team to the congregation. Church leaders suggested that Marty, who had pastored the church for seven years, would lead the worship team. His presence gave a measure of reassurance to older folks who were somewhat fearful of the change.

Along with the introduction of contemporary worship songs, Marty gradually introduced other changes in the worship service including an expanded time of congregational prayer. The worship team worked with Marty and Rayma (the church organist) on providing reverent and timely transitions between the various elements of the worship service.

The congregation reacted well to these changes and received them with relatively little difficulty. The church soon became known regionally for its vibrant and blended style of worship. Key elements contributing to this successful change included prayer, thorough discussion between Marty and the church leaders, careful communication to the congregation at each stage of the change, and a gentle, reverent style of musical presentation.

Similar changes in worship style did not go as smoothly at Faith Baptist Church of Park Rapids, Minnesota (population 3,000), where Marty now serves as pastor. This congregation remained traditional in its worship style throughout its first 30 years of existence. The primary musical instruments included organ and piano, supplemented by a variety of vocal and instrumental selections. The congregation confined its singing to a somewhat dated hymnbook and a smaller book of choruses from the 1970s. Transitions within the worship service were usually informal and choppy. The church's high standards of musical performance reflected the considerable talent found within the congregation.

However, as the congregation grew larger and younger, an increasing number of new attenders approached Marty requesting a more contemporary worship style. In response, Marty met with leaders, and after prayer and discussion, they approved a change in worship style to include the formation of a worship team and the presentation of contemporary worship choruses in a blended service.

With the approval of church leaders Marty selected a worship team and selected a target date for the launch of the new style of worship. As in his former church, Marty preached a series of messages on worship aimed at providing a biblical base. The congregation responded well to the sermon series.

The worship team included vocalists, electronic keyboard, guitars, and drums. The music committee and trustees worked together in expanding the church's sound system to accommodate the needs of the worship team.

Marty met with the worship team leader and briefed the team on the need for a cautious and sensitive presentation of this new style of worship. Marty directed that the team position itself to the right of the speaker's platform in an area previously occupied by the choir. It seemed to Marty that everything was in place for a successful launch.

However, the day prior to the launch, the leader of the worship team determined that it would be more effective for the team to sing from the speaker's platform. She reset the instruments and microphones with this new location in mind. Also, the team determined that they could more effectively minister to newcomers through an enthusiastic, up-tempo presentation that included audience participation.

On the following Sunday morning it was evident that the congregation was not prepared to respond to the multiple changes encompassed in the worship team's approach. They were standing on the speaker's platform (wrong place). Their presentation was high-energy and high-volume (wrong style, especially for the initial transition). And the worship leader—a young woman (for some, wrong gender)—made it clear that she expected them to actively participate in standing, singing, and clapping their hands. The worship team's first Sunday was nearly its last.

After an apology to church leadership, Marty took steps to move the team back to the original location. The team agreed to turn down the volume. And the team leader agreed to select worship choruses that were more subdued. Marty re-clarified with the worship team the reasons for a more gradual transition in worship style.

Unfortunately, the debut of the team had caused significant damage. With Marty's encouragement, church leaders agreed to allow the team to continue under the agreed upon guidelines. However, a subsequent tug of war ensued among the congregation. Some younger attenders clearly preferred what they had heard on that first Sunday. Many older members served notice that, if what they heard that first Sunday was what they would hear every Sunday, they would not continue to attend the church.

It took two years for the worship team to regain credibility. And, while the church has now embraced the new style, a few remain unhappy about the change.

Marty and others in the church learned a number of lessons through what proved to be a difficult process of leading through change: (1) Do not underestimate the importance of context when initiating change. Factors like the placement of the team in the sanctuary and a lack of sensitivity in presentation are magnified under the stress of change. (2) The attitude of the initiators of change matters greatly. In this case, the congregation interpreted insensitivity on the part of the worship team leader as authoritarian and confrontational. They responded negatively. (3) The transition process is as important as the change itself. (4) Clear communication to all participants in the change is crucial. Marty says that he might have prevented much of the pain of this transition by spending more time communicating with the worship team leader and the team members. Assumptions on Marty's part about what the worship team understood were costly in this change process.

Although this was ultimately a good change for the congregation, the process was needlessly painful. However, church leaders can learn much from the mistakes that others have made and avoid unnecessary pain in leading through change in their congregations.

# Building Change

First Baptist Church of Parkers Prairie, Minnesota (population: 900), where Marty served as pastor for a number of years, had met in the same location for 123 years. During the past 10 years the church had tripled in size. However, the church building was landlocked. Every square foot of the property and buildings was being utilized to the fullest extent. Every alternative to relocation had been explored, including multiple services, various remodeling schemes, and moving worship services to the public school. Finally it was becoming clear to even the most devoted old-timers that relocation was the only feasible alternative. Painfully and slowly the decision was made to abandon the existing aging, inadequate facility and build on a new site across town.

The newcomers reacted to the decision with joy, relief, and the attitude: "It's about time!" The old-timers reacted with resignation and reluctance. Clearly both groups needed some assistance in gaining the right perspective on this significant change.

That perspective came when Ruddy and Afton joined their pastor on the platform on a Sunday morning not long after the decision to relocate. These men were brothers whose grandparents had been founding members of the church. After a few words of introduction, Afton spoke of God's blessing and leadership within the church through the years. He remembered prayer meetings and evangelistic services and changed lives. And those who were listening gained a new appreciation for the spiritual work that had been accomplished in this place that was now being left behind.

Then it was Ruddy's turn. Ruddy began to speak softly about his 82 years of experience in the church. He affirmed Afton's recollections of God's blessing and changed lives. The congregation continued to listen with rapt attention.

Then Marty asked Ruddy to tell the congregation about the basement of the church. The basement housed two tiny restrooms, a kitchen, a small storage room, and a fellowship area which, if jam-packed, seated about 80 people. The newcomers had been quite judgmental about the basement of "this old church."

Ruddy's eyes lit up. "Well, it was in the 1930s. Our church didn't have a kitchen, or enough places for Sunday school classes. So a friend and I got together with his horse and wagon, and I crawled into a foundation window well and began to dig with a shovel while laying on my side. My friend hauled away the dirt in his wagon. After quite awhile we finished digging the whole basement and laying up walls of concrete, all without moving the church building. Of course, I was younger then." With a smile, Afton nodded in agreement.

This was a defining moment for the newcomers. With this one gripping story they came to understand what it would take for Ruddy to leave this old building behind. And they better understood what it had cost the old-timers to provide this building that had stood so long.

At the same time, the old-timers were given an example of how they should selflessly be willing to relinquish their emotional ties to the old building, for the sake of future generations. Who among them had invested more in the old building than Ruddy? Yet, by sharing his story, Ruddy was also endorsing the Lord's leading in the move to a new site, a new building, and new opportunities!

Tears were shed that Sunday morning. And more tears were shed when Ruddy was among the first workers at the site for the new church building, a building that he would not live to see completed.

# Adding a Worship Service

The Walnut Grove Christian Church of rural Arcola, Illinois (population 2500), where Barney has ministered for more than 20 years, had a happy problem. Its Sunday morning attendance was larger than its seating capacity. Even with children's church and a nursery, there were few seats left for the church service. Expense and the unavailability of land ruled out building or remodeling. The only way to provide adequate seating was to add a service.

To effect the change, the congregation followed the steps outlined in this book. They prayed about what to do. They studied the community and found that, while many people needed to be working by 10:00 a.m. on Sunday, no church was currently offering a service earlier than that. The leaders read books on adding a service and visited similar congregations that had recently made this change, learning about the benefits and pitfalls.

Through this time of study and discussion, two objections surfaced. The first concerned staffing: it would take twice as many musicians and other workers. While the church leaders realized this might stretch some volunteers a bit, they decided the benefits were worth the effort. The second objection was stronger and was rooted in the agrarian nature of the church: Folks were concerned about personal relationships, saying, "We won't see everyone each week." This concern was voiced repeatedly until finally one of the leaders said, "No, we may not see everyone each week, and that may be what it costs for more people to see Jesus each week." With this, the leaders reached a consensus to start the additional service, doing what they could to minimize the interference with personal relationships.

Following the decision to add a service, the church took several months to plan the details. The congregation was accustomed to having Sunday school at 9:30 with a worship service at 10:30. Realizing their preacher has trouble staying on schedule, they planned the additional service to begin at 8:00, thereby leaving the time between 9:00 and 9:30 to accommodate any overage.

Coffee and donuts are now served during this half hour before Sunday school, and this allows time for those who come to different services to visit with one another. The depth of fellowship has actually improved through this. Whereas people used to offer a quick, superficial greeting before or after the service, now they have time to share prayer needs and other encouragement. The planners also decided to make the two services as similar as possible so that when folks who attended different services during the week discussed what happened, they would be talking about the same service.

Advertising was also a component of the detailed planning. The new service was broadly announced in the community as a "Come as you need to be" service. Worshipers were encouraged to come dressed for work, the lake, Grandma's house, or wherever they were headed after church. In the spring it's not uncommon to see a tractor or two hitched to planters in the church parking lot, ready to head to the field when church is over.

Not only has the addition of a service solved the space problem by effectively doubling the worship seating capacity, both services continue to grow. Instead of damaging personal relationships, the fellowship time between the first service and Sunday school has deepened them, allowing more time for people to visit and share concerns.

# Adding Staff

Sometimes a church makes a long, careful, considered decision to add a staff member. Sometimes God moves in mysterious ways. Walnut Grove Christian Church has experienced both.

One cold December evening the congregation gathered for its annual business meeting. The required reports were given, the nominated officers were elected, and the moderator asked, as usual, if there was any more business before he adjourned the meeting. A mother with teenagers said, "I think we need to hire a youth minister to work with our kids." There were a couple of minutes of discussion, mostly in support. Someone made a motion. A vote was taken. The congregation had decided to add a staff member. This decision was not driven by the leaders. It was not the result of a long study. It just happened.

The church solicited applicants from the student body of a nearby Bible college. One was selected. The church had a new staff member.

Admittedly, the selection process wasn't quite that simple, but the decision to add a staff member was. It went from no prior consideration to approval in less than 10 minutes. The staff position created was only part-time, and the church had adequate financial resources to do this without much concern. Major issues, such as selection, salary, and housing needed to be addressed, but they fell into place with such ease that everyone sensed the Lord was clearing the path. The staff member chosen stayed with the congregation six years and set the standards for future youth ministers.

Later, when the youth minister position was open, the congregation searched extensively for a replacement, contacting dozens of candidates, but could not find one suited to the position. In the interim, one of the volunteer youth workers in the church kept the program going. This young man was self-employed and could fit youth activities into his work schedule. After months of unsuccessful searching for a replacement, one Sunday morning three different members, without any knowledge of the others' thoughts, approached Barney and suggested that the church hire this volunteer leader instead of someone from the outside. This turned out to be a good solution, but, again, it was not the result of careful planning by the leaders—it was the leading of the Holy Spirit.

As the congregation grew, the youth minister position became more than a part-time staff member could handle, and the leaders decided it was time to create a full-time position. This time there was a careful study of the current needs and long-range goals, and thorough planning for the costs of salary, benefits, and programming. Individual leaders were consulted one-on-one. The leaders looked to other similar congregations to see how they handled such decisions. The proposal to hire a full-time staffer was presented to the congregation for its approval. A committee conducted a nationwide search for qualified candidates and interviewed several, and the congregation formally approved the one selected. Prayer came before, during, and after the process. A year after the position was created, the leaders conducted a careful evaluation. This process also resulted in the addition of a good staff member, but it was much more intentional than either of the other two.

We share with you these true stories of change because we don't want you to think that we are advocating that every change needs to happen exactly as we have outlined in this book. Changes can certainly happen in unusual, unplanned, and unexpected ways. The truth is that few changes will be completely textbook in how they happen. We don't believe God is confined to a rigid pattern or several-step method when it comes to bringing change to His church.